A Pilot's Memoirs –

From The Ground Up

Nicholas Gravino Jr.
Captain Delta Air Lines, ret.

Library of Congress Cataloging-in-Publication Data is available on file.

ISBN-13: 978-0-615-24099-2

A Pilot's Memoirs—
From The Ground Up

By Nicholas Gravino Jr.
Captain, Delta Air Lines, ret.

A view of one's sojourn through the aviation industry from one who did it all.

Where, oh where but in *America*. This is truly an American Fairy Tale, which consists of a typical scenario of the *American Dream*, in which the sky is the limit and there are no constraints on what one can do or accomplish here in America the Beautiful… **GOD BLESS AMERICA**. Our founding fathers and those who gave their lives, so that we may pursue and maintain "The Impossible Dream" have bequeathed endless opportunities to us.

My flying career spanned a period of thirty-nine years of flawless flying for a total of 23,130 hours or a total of 10,408,500 miles, which equates to the distance from the Earth to the Moon and back twenty-three and one half times. How many professionals in a given profession can honestly say that their performance lives up to those impeccable standards? Many individuals, both male and female, have the desire to fly, however, only about ten percent have the ability and tenacity to pursue this venue as a career. Anyone can obtain a private pilot's license; however how many of you have the chutzpah to go all the way? I am quite proud of my nephew/Godson, Major Gary John Penna, US Air Force, who chose flying over chemical engineering, his father's profession.

As an aircraft commander, you are required to maintain your physical, mental and emotional abilities "far beyond those of mortal men." You are taught not to push the envelope to the max be it physical, mental or mechanical, as depicted in the motion picture, "Top Gun." You are taught to analyze and evaluate everything and every second that transpires while in command of your aircraft, crew and passengers. Everyone second-guesses your decisions; however, they are not there and do not have all the facts, yet you are held accountable to their decisions, as in the case of the N.T.S.B. (National Transportation Safety Board). At times, their decisions are sheer conjecture and off the wall, as evidenced by the TWA 800 disaster findings. The requirements are mind-boggling. One of your sixth senses is known as "blind trust." This is the ability, not only of the captain but the entire crew who must rely upon every individual, both seen and un-seen, who is involved with your particular flight, which might include, "The butcher, baker and the candlestick maker." They must perform their assigned tasks with sheer perfection. There is no room for error or miscalculation. It is the responsibility of the captain, and only the captain, to question anything and everything that appears contrary to normal operating procedures and then some to ensure that everyone does his job in an impeccable fashion. In the final analysis he or she is the one in command and fully responsible, come hell or high water.

Many of today's professionals seek the easy way out, make impressive salaries, negotiate golden parachutes with all kinds of perks and make an occasional decision. Piloting an aircraft, on the other hand, can be difficult where split second decisions have to be made, post haste. These decisions have to be precise with no room for error while everyone is breathing down your neck. You screw up; it is called *"Pilot Error"....* you are maligned for the rest of your life and beyond. Yes, there are cases of pilot error; however, no one really knows what the total circumstances were at the time (those split seconds prior to impact) when the decision had to be made that affected the result. Flying an aircraft can become an impossible task at times; it is quite precise and an unforgiving, thankless profession that is severely scrutinized and criticized. Everyone, "Monday

Morning Quarterbacks" and everyone becomes an expert on something that they know little about. I, however, have, "been there and done that" and as the title suggests, *"From The Ground Up."* There is no physical evidence of your accomplishments afterwards except for the smiling faces of family members or friends at their reunions. Unfortunately, these reunions are not visible in today's world, because of the threat of terrorism and its subsequent security requirements; no visitors allowed, however, they do exist.

Dedication

I would like to dedicate this offering to my two wonderful daughters, Linda Anne and Leslie Anne and their mother Elaine and my grandsons, Michael James and Thomas Nicholas

I would also like to dedicate this offering to
Pat "Mother" Malone, Captain Angus Perry and Captain Pete Loranger, who believed in me and nurtured me during my thirty-year career. Everything that I have accomplished, I owe to them.

I would also like to mention all the men and women of previous generations and in today's world of aviation and thank them for the contributions that came from their fruits of labor.

Acknowledgments

I thank the late Captain Roland O. Loranger, Chief Pilot Delta Air Lines/Northeast Airlines and the late H. Angus Perry, Flight Instructor and Line Check Airmen Delta Air Lines/Northeast Airlines and also Pat Mother Malone, Simulator Instructor, for believing in me and guiding me throughout my career.

I thank Captain Ray Lahr, United Air Lines, retired, for his evaluation and contributions to the TWA 800 Disaster. Captain Lahr is in the process of taking the NTSB to court, in an attempt to correct the NTSB's off the wall explanation of the TWA 800 Disaster.

Thanks to Captain Larry Pullen, Delta Air Lines, ret. famous aviation photographer, for allowing me to use his photograph for the cover of my book; it is very apropos, as, this is "from the ground up." Mr. Alberto Riva of Milan, Italy for granting the permission to utilize his exceptional photo of a Delta Air Lines B767 ER (Extended Range) landing at New York International Airport.

Thanks to Glenn McDonald and his wife Barbara, who were along as passengers on my last flight. Also to Ms. Dorothy Frances in editing and helping me make sense to this gibberish.

Honorable mention goes to Ms. Barbara Chiaverini of Yonkers, N.Y. a stewardess for Northeast Airlines of whom I became quite fond of and who is no longer with us.

Foreword

I've written this autobiographical sketch as a dedicated individual who has devoted his life and love for aviation to an illustrious career. Everything contained in this book is from my point of view and my view only, so please bear with me. My main objective in writing this book is to enlighten and expose, rather than lecture the concerned public, be they airline traveler, aircraft gazer, flight student (private or military) male or female, child to senior citizen or anyone else in between. It pertains to the inner most operations of the airline industry, its personnel and all other entities associated with transporting Jack and Jill from point A to point B, safe and sound.

"These are a few of my favorite things"

I, Nicholas Gravino Jr., was born May 25, 1936 in Jamaica, Queens, NY, a second generation Italian who loves his ethnicity, his religion, and his realistic values. I attended public schools, but never attended a formal university because of the lack of the financial where with all or the proper guidance due to the need to support my family during trying times. I fell in love with aviation at the early age of three, and with the Grace of God, did the right thing and positioned myself to be in the right place at the right time to build a more than comfortable life for myself and my family. I served my country honorably in the United States Navy during the waning days of the Korean Conflict and I am a very dedicated American Citizen. I love my country dearly and for what it stands. I worked my way through civilian flight schools while supporting my family when my parents were quite ill. This will be a walk down memory lane together, through the eyes of one who has *"been there, done that"* the hard way. I hope you enjoy this collage as much as I have enjoyed reminiscing *"days gone by"*.

Contents

Chapter One:

A Flashback from Last Flight to Pre World War II, to December 06, 1941

There I was commanding my last flight; the date was May 19, 1996 and I was, as ground school instructor Al Costa would say, "flying along in flight". I just engaged the autopilot at my cruising altitude of thirty-three thousand feet over the Swiss Alps. On this crystal day off my right wing I could see the base and peak of the Matterhorn. I had another 7 hours 22 minutes ahead of me from Milan, Italy to New York's Kennedy Airport, where it all began for me at my birth in nearby South Ozone Park, some fifty-nine years and three hundred and fifty-eight days prior. It would be the end of my illustrious career at an estimated time of arrival, (ETA) of 14:52 eastern daylight savings time. I mused over the different junctures of my career. I could only think about the numerous stops along the way and all that had occurred. I had to force myself to concentrate on my flying and not my past, since my two captain qualified first officers John Grossweiler and Guy Gerard, refused to fly the trip back. They said that this was my day in the sun and they did not want to rain on my parade, while the *visions of aviation sugarplums danced in my head.*" All I could think about were the events associated with all my childhood fantasies that came true and that my last landing had better be a good one and that I had better not screw it up. Incidentally, regardless of what transpires during a flight, it is the landing the crew is critiqued on. My love affair with this airplane, the B767 ER (extended -range) began for me in January of 1993. I felt very comfortable and confident with this particular Boeing product, as well as

1

all other Boeing products that I have had the privilege to command, as the saying goes "Boeing builds them better." I flew Boeings from 1967 to 1996 without ever having a major problem, zero engine failures, bird strikes, wind shear, etc. The B767 was far superior to the Airbus A310. This was my last flight, the termination of my career as an airline driver, which spanned some thirty-nine years. I remember saying to myself, "Self, you've come a long way, son, and don't you forget it." As I sat there doing my job, going through the motions, I could not help but think of the charmed life I had led, all the great people I had met and came to love…. how I came to be where I am today, on this day of days.

In retrospect, my parents were first generation Italian-Americans whose parents legally immigrated here from Naples and Sicily during the rush of the early nineteen hundreds, arriving under the watchful eyes and gentle care of Lady Liberty at the entrance of New York Harbor. During the developmental years of my life, my paternal grandmother Rose wanted me to become a priest. I did consider the priesthood at one point in my life, however, aviation won out. Nanna Rose has to be a saint. She lived a very demanding life here in America, raised three children, picked and planted vegetables on the farms at Aqueduct Race Track for a mere twenty-five cents an hour. She couldn't speak English but never lost her faith in the Catholic religion or in freedom here in America. My maternal grandfather, Giuseppi however, was a majestic man who was in the Italian Calvary prior to, "***Coming to America***". I can still envision the portrait of him mounted upon his stallion in his military uniform; it looked like a scene from the Student Prince. He was a musician, played the accordion and was the adhesive that kept the family together during the trying times of WWII. My family presented him with an accordion on his sixtieth birthday and he was in tears. He would play all the Italian folk songs, some from operas of Verdi and Puccini. He taught us kids a great deal pertaining to our Italian heritage. His death was untimely in 1962 and I still miss him.

I lived in South Ozone Park, which is in the borough of Queens, New York. It is the last hamlet before entering New York International Airport, aka, JFK, alias Idlewild. Not only was I born there, I grew up there, went to school there, played there, witnessed the airport being built, I worked on the ground there, I flew there, and I retired there.

Now, return with me to yesteryear and fasten your seat belts.

My introduction to aviation came in 1939 at the New York World's Fair when I was exposed to the "World of Tomorrow." The Trilon-Perisphere was the logo of the World's Fair. Exhibits consisted of homes, industries, planes, and trains of the twentieth century and beyond. I have many fond recollections of the General Motors exhibition. I was even more impressed with the Goodyear exhibition, which included a model of the Goodyear Blimp. I remember the "City of Tomorrow," a Train Exhibition, which I just discovered was presented by the Pennsylvania Railroad System. I was very fascinated with the aviation exhibits, encompassing the airliners of the future. Unfortunately, the 1939 World's Fair was terminated prematurely at the outbreak of World War II. Did you know that prior to the outbreak of the war, Japan purchased all our scrap iron and utilized it in the building of their war machine?

As a child, I recall traveling to the LaGuardia Marine Air Terminal to view the Boeing 314, the Pan American four-engine flying boat that was the focal point of Ken Follett's intriguing novel, "Night Over Water." These graceful swans would taxi on to the waters surrounding LaGuardia Airport and take off at Port Washington on Long Island Sound. It was quite an inspiring sight of yesteryear, especially for me.

I remember living near the Belt Parkway under the approach path to a small airport known as Jamaica Sea & Land. I would look to the sky and see these beautiful and graceful Piper J3 Cubs, consisting of a sixty-five horsepower engine, metal tubing and covered with Irish linen and painted in a brilliant yellow lacquer with a black lightning bolt on the side of the fuselage. The Cub climbed, cruised and descended at 60 MPH.

The Piper J3 Cub would become the mainstay of my flying career in September of 1957.

As a child, I listened to numerous serial radio programs, prior to TV, like Buck Rogers and Flash Gordon. Incidentally, Buster Crabbe, an Olympic swimmer and star of Flash Gordon had his picture taken with me at the World's Fair. I would also listen to, and eventually watch, Sky King with his nephew and niece, Clipper and Penny, originally in his twin engine Cessna T50 "Bamboo Bomber," which was replaced with a Cessna 310 for the TV series.

About ten miles southwest of my home was the naval air station called "Floyd Bennett Field," named for Lieutenant Commander Richard Byrd's personal pilot when he flew over the North Pole. My father worked there during WWII with the beaching crew for the US Navy sea planes, including the PBY Flying Boats, OS2U, "Kingfisher" and PBM's, just to name a few.

One other thing that impressed me as a young child was that Charles Lindberg utilized Roosevelt Field as his jumping off point to "The Unknown World of Trans-Ocean Aerial Navigation." Roosevelt Field was turned into a gigantic shopping mall and now houses an Aviation Museum, known as **The Cradle of Aviation.** The 1950's movie, "The Spirit of St. Louis," was filmed at Zahn's Airport, Amityville, Long Island. I took my first flying lesson there at Amityville Flight Service from a Long Island aviation pioneer named Ed Lyons.

The only major airport at that time in New York was LaGuardia Airport in Elmhurst, Queens. Initially, it was called the Glenn Curtis Airport, in honor of the aviation pioneer. Eventually the name was changed to North Beach Airport and then LaGuardia, in honor of then Mayor Fiorello LaGuardia, a colorful Italian. There was a tiny private airport about a mile East of LaGuardia known as Flushing Airport run by a tyrant named Speed Hanslick, who would chain your airplane to the pavement, if you did not pay your bills.

The major International Airport was in Newark, NJ. Construction at LaGuardia was started in 1937 and entailed an enormous amount of fill, which caused major problems during construction and in the years to come. LaGuardia Airport would inherit the name, "La Garbage" due to the settling, decomposition and stench of the fill material at low tide. The six hangars were constructed on pilings, which were bored and pounded to the point of refusal. Eventually, the area around them had to be rebuilt, due to settling. When a major construction project of new terminals in the 1960's and 1970,s was in progress, many extra pilings had to be inserted because of the buried debris, namely car bodies. I remember landing at LaGuardia on numerous occasions and thinking that we had a malfunction of the air-conditioning system in the airplane. In actuality, it was the odor from the buried fills of the 1930,s.

I was quite inquisitive as a child. I loved to listen to radio waves and aeronautical broadcasts. I'd sit on my bed, listening to my radio and soon discovered that when I tuned an AM radio dial below 550 KC's (Kilocycles). I would receive the following in Morse Code: dah dit, dit dit dit, dah dit dah dit… which, when translated into English were the letters "NSC," the Morse Code call sign for Naval Air Station New York or Floyd Bennett Field. On occasion, I would hear the NAS air traffic control tower talking to the aircraft on the low frequency radio band. *"These are some of the things"* that occupied my early life prior to WWII and piqued my interest in *"the wild blue yonder."*

Chapter Two:

World War II, December 07, 1941 to September 02, 1945

I Am sure everyone my age remembers that the outbreak of World War II occurred on a sleepy Sunday morning at 07:55 AM Honolulu time, 12:55 New York time. I remember it vividly. It was customary in our New York Italian household that we were required to spend Sunday afternoons at my maternal grandfather's home. My grandfather was considered The Don; however, he was quite aristocratic, patriotic and had no resemblance to Don Corleone of "The Godfather" fame. Turacamo Paving, Inc., an Italian paving contractor in New York City, employed my maternal grandfather, as a paving supervisor. He worked until age 72. Every Sunday was just like a scene from, "The Godfather" only thirty-one years earlier or at the same time frame of the movie. It was a gathering of the Clan Macaluso, my mother's maiden name. It gave us the opportunity to visit with all our aunts, uncles, and cousins. My mother had three brothers and two sisters and I had twelve cousins. All the cousins were so close that even to this day, I consider them to be my brothers and sisters.

The big attraction was to sit in my grandfather's living room and listen to his gigantic eighteen vacuum tube radio, which included some short wave bands. We played musical instruments and games. The men played bocce, drink beer and played cards. The women cooked Italian food and my grandfather supplied steaks and sausages along with home-grown tomatoes, peppers, lettuce and numerous other vegetables from his garden. My grandfather shopped at an Italian outdoor farmers market in the Bronx, known as Hunt's Point and purchase various cheeses and pastries. On **"The Day That Will Live in Infamy,"** we kids were playing "Fat Dumb and Happy," not knowing that the next hour would change our lives and our families forever. At approximately 14:00, EST (Eastern Standard Time), there was an interruption of all radio broadcasts with the horrific news that the Japanese had destroyed our naval fleet on battleship row in Pearl Harbor.

Even though I was only five years old, I had a keen sense of the ramifications of a World War based on my previous studies of WWI. I had been fascinated with the World War I flying aces, Rickenbacker, Doolittle and Baron Von Richthofen plus the aircraft, which consisted of Jennys, Spads, Sopwith Camels and the likes. Incidentally, there is an airport in Rhinebeck, NY that recreates the air war over Europe during WWI. It is quite thrilling. When the news broke, everyone was crying; my uncles were in their twenties and early thirties and knew they would be called to serve their country. My father was classified 4F, due to a punctured eardrum. My uncle Charley, Karl T. Hallberg was to become my idol and mentor. He enlisted in the US Army Air Corps and became a P-47 fighter pilot for the Ninth Air Force, 366th Fighter Group, 389th Fighter Squadron based in England and eventually in Asch, Belgium during the Battle of the Bulge. He was involved in a near fatal mishap, on which I will elaborate in a later chapter.

My uncle Mac, the oldest Macaluso at thirty-two, was drafted and stationed on New Guinea in the Pacific with the Army Corps of Engineers. He was married but had no children. My Uncle Tom, a Gravino, enlisted in the US Navy as an aviation machinist mate and was stationed in the Panama Canal Zone and Coco Beach, Florida. He is a great guy, and I truly appreciate what he did for me during my early years. He is now eighty-five years old and living in Palm Beach, Florida with his wife, Gloria...a second cousin to Rudy Giuliani.

I remember practicing air raid drills in grade school and listening to Mayor Fiorello LaGuardia read the comic strips to the children, which was a Sunday morning radio ritual during newspaper strikes in New York. I had an uncle who was an Air Raid Warden. He had a white helmet, a la World War One and an armband with a CD on it, signifying Civil Defense, a flashlight and a pump type watering can to extinguish fires... lots of luck. We attended war bond drives, went to the movies where they took up collections and watched Movie Tone news reels pertaining to the war in Europe and the Pacific.

On June 13, 1943, I attended an Italian feast in honor of St. Anthony of Padua, which was the patron saint of the church that I attended. It was a Sunday afternoon at 15:00. My friends and I got together, had some Italian food and pastries, listened to music and played games. I was near the outer confines of the feast when two olive drab US Army troop transport trucks arrived with covered canvas tops and sides. Two MPs exited from each truck with side arms and rolled up the canvas tarps at the rear of the trucks, exposing Italian prisoners of war with a P on their fatigue uniforms. The prisoners of war were permitted to roam the feast. The elderly Italian women hugged and kissed these prisoners and purchased food on their behalf. These were our enemy. I was only seven years old at the time, but it just blew my mind that these women treated the enemy as conquering heroes. This was against my patriotic beliefs. I still cannot understand it.

We had some great military leaders during that crisis who were born and placed in the right place at the right time. They included our president, Franklin Delano Roosevelt, who rallied this country and the world to do its part for the war effort and then some. The combination of Franklin Delano Roosevelt and Harry S. Truman, a haberdasher from Missouri, was the perfect team to defeat the Axis Powers. Harry's mantra was *"The Buck Stops here,"* which is non-existent in today's political world. He went down in history for giving the order to drop the atomic bomb on Japan, which took a lot of guts and soul searching. In my estimation, the only other president with that caliber of fortitude to come down the pike was Ronald Reagan. Another individual who deserves honorable mention during World War II was Winston S. Churchill, who led the British Empire through the most devastating times at the hands of the Nazis. The Holocaust, inflicted by the Nazis against the Jews, took its toll upon my love for humanity. In later years, I visited the home of Anne Frank in Amsterdam and it was quite heart wrenching.

As far as the military goes, we had the likes of Eisenhower, Marshall, Patton, Bradley and Hap Arnold in Europe. In the Pacific, we had MacArthur, Nimitz, Halsey, Doolittle and General Wainwright. Who could ever forget the movies that came out of the war years? There was "Thirty Seconds Over Tokyo," which focused on the April 18, 1942, Jimmy Doolittle raid with Mitchell B-25 bombers that were launched from the aircraft carrier Hornet some 600 miles off the coast of Japan as seen through the eyes of Ted Lawson, an aircraft commander played by Van Johnson. It was also filmed in a recent movie entitled, "Pearl Harbor," starring Ben Affleck, Josh Hartnett, Cuba Gooding Jr. and Kate Beckinsale. It was a little far fetched... but good it tugged at your heartstrings. There were so many other movies, such as "They Were Expendable," pertaining to the PT boats that took General MacArthur from the Philippines to Australia, starring Duke Wayne and Robert Montgomery. There was a movie many years later entitled "Swing Shift," starring...Goldie Hawn and Kurt Russell, depicting a love affair that developed in a defense plant during WWII.

There were so many other movies that piqued our interest in the war uniting us to support the war effort, regardless of race, color or creed. Again, this is something that is non-existent in today's world. Many of the Hollywood stars assumed the roles of service men and women who fought for our country and its beliefs. They did not question our dedication to freedom as Hollywood does today. There were superstars in the field of journalism, too, including Ernie Pyle, Edward R. Murrow and Walter Cronkite, just to name a few. They reported the news and did not influence or interpret the news. They gave us the opportunity to judge for ourselves. Incidentally, Ernie Pyle was killed while reporting the news on April 18, 1945 on the island of Le Shima. A movie was made about his life entitled "The Story of G.I. Joe," with Burgess Meredith and Robert Mitchum. There was also LIFE and LOOK magazines, which gave us a blow-by-blow description of the on-going battles in Europe and the Pacific. The magazine covers won all kind of awards. There were the famous paintings of Norman Rockwell in the SATURDAY EVENING POST that truly depicted *Every-town USA during the war years.*

Early in the war, there was an incident that occurred at midnight on June 13, 1942 on the eastern end of Long Island in the sleepy little hamlet of Amagansett. A German submarine surfaced and deposited four German saboteurs. The saboteurs lived in the US and three were naturalized citizens. They were eventually captured in New York City. Two were executed, and two were sent to prison; President Truman commuted their sentences in 1948 and they were deported.

When thinking back to World War II my first grade teacher, Mrs. Duncan comes to mind. She would bring in to class on Monday, the New York Herald Tribune Sunday colored comic section which included the pictures, medals and description of our men and leaders in uniform. I learned about Pappy Boyington, Joe Foss, Francis Gabreski, Jimmy Doolittle, Ira Hayes and Renee Gagnon. Incidentally, Hayes and Gagnon were two of the US Marines who raised the flag on Iwo Jima. Following World War II, I was fortunate to meet Pappy Boyington, of the Black Sheep Squadron. I have a signed picture of him and his airplane on the wall in my den. I also met Renee Gagnon who was an employee of Northeast Airlines in Lebanon, NH. I met Paul Tibbets, the pilot of the Enola Gay, of "atomic bomb" fame. Ensign Gay, who fought in the Battle of Midway, was shot down and viewed the battle in the water from a raft. One of the saddest stories that came out of WWII was the loss of the five Sullivan brothers on the same ship in the US Navy. The five brothers were seamen onboard the USS Juneau during the Battle of Guadalcanal, which was destroyed on November 13, 1942 by two torpedoes from a Japanese sub. Because of that tragedy, FDR declared that no relatives would be allowed to serve on the same ship.

My Uncle Charley, Lt. Karl T. Hallberg, US Army Air Corps, flew P-47 Republic Thunderbolts in Europe and eventually was stationed at an airbase with a designator of Y29 in Asch, Belgium. It was there on December 31, 1944 that he and three other P47s took off on a mission during the Battle of the Bulge. Their mission was to seek and destroy targets of opportunity, namely German trains and troop movements. The P-47 was equipped with two 500-pound bombs, under each wing. My uncle went in for a bomb run and for some unknown reason the bomb under the right wing would not release. He tried desperately to shake the bomb loose by sawing the rudder back and forth with the rudder pedals, in an attempt to dislodge the bomb, to no avail. It was decided he would return to base and attempt to land the aircraft gently, in order to save the aircraft from total destruction. Aircraft was and is a very valuable asset. Upon touch down, the defective bomb released and subsequently exploded. Everything aft of his bucket seat on the aircraft was destroyed and his eight fifty-caliber machine gun magazines exploded. The shrapnel from the bomb destroyed the aircraft. Miraculously, my uncle survived with a head injury. An eyewitness stated that he staggered out of the cockpit, rolled off the wing, and lost consciousness. Subsequent to the mishap, he resumed his duties as a fighter pilot with the 9th Air Force. A picture that I proudly display on my wall is in the archives at the Smithsonian Institute, the Air Force Museum at Wright Patterson Air Force Base in Fairborn, OH and The Cradle of Aviation on Long Island, NY and within the archives of Republic Aviation. I gave the name "Miraculous Metal," to this picture and rightfully so. It was also mentioned in a video entitled, "A Fighter Pilot's Story," by Quentin Aanenson. I viewed the tape on PBS in 1992 and freaked out when I saw his aircraft. I contacted Mr. Aanenson and he confirmed that it was indeed my uncle's aircraft. This man and his daring do nature was my inspiration to seek my place in *The Wild Blue Yonder*.

I have just come across the December 31, 1944 Official Flight Operations Log of the 389th Fighter Squadron of the 9th Air Force, 366th Fighter Group, which I include for your reading. This log was provided by my cousin, Joseph Zagorski, Jr., who was quite close to our uncle Charley and who attends all 366th Fighter Group reunions. The Flight Operations Log reads as follows:

> *Lieutenant Hallberg has been judged the luckiest man in the squadron, an honor he will probably retain permanently. For on the last day of the month, when landing from the first mission of the day, a hung bomb dropped off the plane and exploded. The accident tore the airplane into bits, as far forward as the armor plate, yet Lt. Hallberg was able to climb out on to the wing before losing consciousness. His head was severely cut in the back and he was hospitalized for complete recovery, but otherwise uninjured.*

He suffered severe headaches for the remainder of his life, because of the metal plate inserted in his head.

During the war, I attended P.S. 96 in Queens. We had war bond drives and various other activities to promote the war effort. In one of these drives, the male faculty of the school, including Mr. Nielsen, the custodian, constructed a skeletal wooden replica of a Navy Grumman F4F Wildcat that was put on display. This blew my mind. I sat on a makeshift bucket seat and pretended that I was taking off from the aircraft carrier Yorktown, somewhere in the Pacific. I remember that the first balsa stick and tissue paper airplane that I constructed was a Bell P-39 Air Cobra, which had a 20 mm cannon mounted in the prop spinner of the nose.

I played fighter pilot with my cousin Joey and my sister Rosemarie. We sat on a staircase in our home and I had a knapsack on my back, pretending it was a parachute; my sister had a make- believe first-aid kit. We pretended I was the aircraft commander, Joey was my co-pilot and my sister Rosemarie was the nurse. Our mission was to rescue downed flyers in the Pacific Ocean in our PBY Amphibian.

Every Wednesday during the war, the entire school attended an assembly in the auditorium. Male students were required to wear white dress shirts and ties, female students wore blouses … the color guard would wear red, white and blue sashes; it was very inspiring and patriotic.

During one of the bond rallies sponsored by the U.S. Army, if you purchased a $25 bond you received a ride in a U.S. Army Jeep. My Uncle Tom gave me a sailor suit and I sang the U.S. Coast Guard song. To this day, I still remember the words. For my performance, which I ended with a military salute, I was rewarded with a ride in the infamous Willy's Jeep. The name JEEP originated from the expression, "GP" or general purpose and is still in use today. When we contributed enough bond money to buy a vehicle, we received a plaque with the picture of the vehicle we purchased; it would then be displayed on the wall of our grade school. There were also Blood Donor drives.

Many major fighter aircraft were constructed on Long Island. There was Grumman in Bethpage and Calverton, which constructed F4F Wildcats, F6F Hellcats, TBF Avenger and F7F Bearcats. Republic Aircraft in Farmingdale constructed the P47 Thunderbolt or as it was commonly known, the Jug, because it was almost impossible to destroy. My uncle can attest to that. There was also Curtis Wright in Valley Stream, Long Island, which constructed the P40, Warhawk, made famous by the "Flying Tigers" of General Chenault and John Wayne in the movie by the same name. Many dedicated women assumed the roles of "Rosie the Riveter" or "Wanda the Welder." Rosie and Wanda relieved their male counterparts to go to war and it kept the assembly lines operating 24/7/365.

My Aunt Mary helped to construct troop gliders for the US Army Air Force, which were used during the D-Day invasion of Normandy. Another outfit that deserves honorable mention was the black air corps pilot group of the then unknown "Tuskegee Airmen," flying North American P-51 Mustangs to escort the B17 bombers over Germany. There are so many other groups and individuals who paid the ultimate sacrifice, of whom I am personally unaware; however, I salute them all.

There was a US Army base known as Camp Upton in Yaphank, Long Island, now Brookhaven National Laboratory, which was instrumental in developing the Atomic Bomb. Incidentally, Irving Berlin was there during WWI and wrote a tune entitled "Yip, Yip Yaphank" for one of his Broadway shows. He also wrote, "This is the Army Mr. Jones," and especially, "God Bless America." There was also Fort Dix in New Jersey and McGuire Air Base.

I remember riding one Saturday afternoon during the summer near Mitchell Field, a U.S. Army Air Corps field in Nassau County, Long Island and witnessing a two ship landing formation of the Lockheed P38 Lightening. This was a twin engine, single seat pursuit plane with two liquid-cooled engines with counter rotating propellers to reduce the effects of torque on takeoff. It was an awesome display of airmanship and to this day, I can still see them coming over that fence at about twenty feet above the car.

Luxury liners were pressed into service; the Queen Mary, Queen Elizabeth, Britannic, Mauritania, Normandie, and the Il De France... to transport troops to foreign countries to topple the "Dastardly Acts of Aggression," to quote FDR.

I would travel to the Brooklyn Piers or the Brooklyn Navy Yard and view the liberty ships being loaded and built for the transportation of precious cargo for the Allied Forces in Europe, or to view the construction of aircraft carriers and various other war ships. In years to come, these liberty ships would be anchored up the Hudson River in New York and utilized subsequent to the war to store grain, which would eventually be sold to Russia. My father was a welder at the Brooklyn Navy Yard and my uncle Dominick was a pipe fitter who worked at these defense plants during the war, constructing these guardians of the deep.

An incident I recollect quite vividly was the fire and sinking of the Normandie, which was docked in New York Harbor on the Hudson River and was being outfitted to become a troop transport. Apparently, a welder ignited some flammable material, which got out of control, causing an enormous amount of water to be poured on the fire, eventually causing the Normandie to capsize at the pier. I remember driving by with a relative and seeing this enormous luxury liner lying on her side. There was speculation that it was sabotage. Eventually it was used as scrap.

I recollect seeing Movie Tone newsreels of ships, planes and tanks being sent via convoys to our allies in Europe under a program entitled, "Lend Lease." This project was the brainchild of FDR and came into existence in March of 1941. FDR set up the Office of Lend Lease, wherein the US would supply the Allies with vital defense equipment, which ultimately was instrumental in the defeat of the Axis Powers in Europe and the Pacific. Without it, Europe would have been defeated prior to D-Day. To this day, not all the Allies have paid America back monetarily for what we did to preserve *Peace on Earth*. This turned out to be just another American give-away program. As the song goes, *The Rich get Richer, The Poor Get Poorer.*

I remember an airplane crash in New York City. It was a Saturday morning, July 28, 1945 at 09:49. A U.S. Army Air Corps Mitchell B25 twin-engine bomber crashed into the 79th floor of the Empire State Building. One of the engines wound up in an elevator shaft and fell with the elevator car to the basement; the safety devices slowed the elevator. Miraculously, the two women in the elevator survived.

I think that there are so many other groups and individuals that I feel should have been mentioned in this book. However, this book is dedicated to those men and women of all nations especially in Korea, Viet Nam, Afghanistan and Iraq who gave and who will give the supreme sacrifice to preserve this wonderful world in which we live.

I would be remiss if I did not give honorable mention to the men and women of the United States Army Air Corps, Air Transport Command, Women's Auxiliary Ferry Squadron (WAFS) and the Women Air Force Service Pilots (WASPs) of World War II.

Women who were pioneers of aviation should be mentioned here also. They were Amelia Earhart, Jacqueline Cochran and Ann B Carl, who later became one of my early flight instructors in the Piper J3 Cub at Zahn's Airport, Amityville NY. I have just learned that Ann B. Carl worked as a test pilot for the Army Air Corps at Wright Field in Fairborn, OH and was the first woman to fly a jet plane. The aircraft was the XP59, Bell Aircomet, which was a far cry from a Piper J3 Cub. It was one of the stick and tissue models that I happened to build.

I met some of those gallant men and women of the Air Transport Command at Northeast Airlines. I remember names like Freddie Lord who was portrayed as "Dooley "in the movie, "Island in the Sky," Clark Willard and Pete Loranger, to name a few. I could go on ad infinitum, as this period represents a major turning point in my life and the formidable years; however, it is time to move on.

Chapter Three:

Post World War II,
September 03, 1945 to June 24, 1949

T he War finally ended with the surrender of Germany and the dropping of the Atomic Bomb on Hiroshima and Nagasaki. The surrender was signed onboard the USS Missouri on Tokyo Bay. The joy and sadness endured for many months and many years, and became an eternity for many. I remember a photo of a sailor kissing a female in Times Square, in which she was in a near horizontal position. It's become a classic. The title of this classic photo is, "Kissing the War Good Bye," A VJ Day poster by Alfred Eisenstaedt, dated August 14, 1945.

There were many festive occasions, which included parades, meeting of returning convoys of ships on both coasts, block parties, closing of defense plants, etc. I remember attending many block parties. There were many movies depicting the adjustments required on the part of our service men from all walks of life, one of which was "The Best Years of Our Lives," starring Fredrick March, Myrna Loy, Dana Andrews, Teresa Wright, Hogey Carmichael and Harold Russell, a US Navy enlisted man, who in reality did lose both his hands. He won an Academy Award as "best supporting actor" for his portrayal of Homer Parrish.

One of the first construction projects subsequent to WWII was John F. Kennedy International Airport, aka New York International Airport, originally known as Idlewild Airport. It was an area of wetlands associated with Jamaica Bay and a wild life preserve. The local area was known as Richmond Hill Circle and was the terminus of the Green Bus

Line Q10. This bus now operates from Kew Gardens, Queens to all the terminals at JFK. I played baseball there as center fielder for the Idlewild Jets in 1951, adjacent to the Belt Parkway and Van Wyck Expressway, the main highways in and out of JFK, at the northern end of the airport on the Belt Parkway. We made it to the championships, of the South Queens Police Athletic League; however, we lost to the Rosedale Trojan's.

Idlewild Airport construction commenced in 1942 and was completed initially in 1947 for the grand opening; the Port Authority of New York & New Jersey (PONYA) operated it. Construction remains in progress, continuously.

In 1947, there was a two-week air show, which I attended as often as permitted. I would also sneak there on my bicycle. They had very impressive static displays that fascinated me no end; one in particular was a vertical cross section of the new jet engines, which consisted of very few moving parts and operated to visualize the jet propulsion process. I remember that the largest aircraft on display was the Boeing B36, which was the predecessor to the B47 and eventually the B52, which is still in existence today. The B36 had a combination of six piston engines with four jet engines and was featured in the movie, "Strategic Air Command" starring Jimmy Stuart and June Allison. They also teamed up in "The Glenn Miller Story." The Lockheed P80 Shooting Star was on display… it was the latest jet fighter of the US Air Force.

Jet engines were in their infancy during this time period and would become the mainstay of the aviation industry in years to come. During the air show, someone was demonstrating the use of a remote controlled propeller drone when it crashed into the flagpole on top of the Green Bus Line maintenance building, just off the Belt Parkway and the 150th Street entrance to the airport. There were only three hangars available at that time, adjacent to runway 13L on the north end of the airport, one in which I worked as an assistant dispatcher and crew scheduler with

Northeast Airlines in the late 1950s. The terminal area consisted of Quonset huts with a three-story mini control tower. This was a far cry from the humongous airport city of today. I eventually worked there as a passenger service representative in 1958.

Lockheed Aircraft opened up a maintenance facility on the airport known as LASI, Lockheed Aircraft Service International. Their job was to repair and maintain World War II type aircraft, the then modern Douglas DC6/DC7 and the Lockheed 049/1049 Constellations. We would sneak over there on our bicycles and invariably get chased. We would stand there in awe admiring these modern day flying machines that had the ability to *"Slip the Surly Bonds of Earth."* On the northern end of the airport, there was a derelict DC3 parked, which was used for fire-fighting. We would climb on board and pretended that we were flying the North Atlantic. The DC3 Dakota, as it was named, became the backbone of the war as a C47 and as a twenty-four passenger aircraft, is still flying today. Auspiciously, it became the first aircraft I would fly during my thirty-and-a-half years with the airlines.

Subsequent to the war, Levitt and Sons, named Levittown, undertook a major home building project that emerged on Long Island, NY. It was tailored for the returning veterans of World War II. GI's were able to purchase a home through the GI Bill of Rights for the sum of $7,990. This trend lasted for decades and spread throughout the entire United States. Incidentally, Levitt and Sons is still in existence today, building in Port St. Lucie, FL at Tradition. My father worked for Levitt & Sons as a carpenter in the 1940s and 1950s. I had relatives reside there until two years ago. The value of the homes increased from $7,990 to $300,000 plus today.

Another project was the formation of the United Nations, which originated from The League of Nations founded by President Woodrow Wilson. The original United Nations Charter was signed in San Francisco in 1945. Initially, the UN was housed in Lake Success on the border of

Queens and Nassau Counties on Long Island, NY. The UN was also housed in the New York State Pavilion at the New York World's Fair Grounds on the Grand Central Parkway, just south of LaGuardia Airport. This now houses the US Open Tennis Stadium, which was originally in Forest Hills, Queens. The UN Headquarters was built on a site on the banks of the East River at Forty-second Street and FDR Drive. It was completed in January of 1951 and remains the headquarters to this day.

The UN has become a major problem due to their lack of decision-making and their failure to support the United States during the Iraq War. In addition, when leaders from foreign countries stay in NY, it creates major problems for America and for New York as a result of heavy security and traffic congestion. I will not belabor the issues, except to say, that we would be a Hell of a lot better off without the UN here in America. In my estimation, the UN is a bane and not a boon. It would behoove us to evict the UN, send it to some third world island in the Pacific off Japan, where it would be less of a target for terrorists, and convert the UN building into a shelter for the homeless in America. What say you? Many of the problems America and the free world face today are due to the inactions and the lackluster attitude of The United Nations Security Council.

The Berlin Airlift came into existence on June 27, 1948 and lasted until May 12, 1949. This was a result of an attempt by the Soviet Union to push the West out of Berlin by stopping all Western movement of supplies to Berlin through Soviet-controlled East Berlin in order to search, causing everything to grind to a halt. Eventually, the Soviet Union stopped all ground activity to Berlin through the Soviet Sector. The Berlin Airlift was approved by President Truman and consisted of an airlift by the free world to provide food, medical supplies, and various other materials to sustain life. Eventually, it became effective against Soviet aggression.

Some notable events televised during this time period was the Senator Joseph McCarthy Senate Investigations into Communism and the Senator Estes Kefauver Crime Commission.

The new media of television treated us to the view of two atomic blasts in the Pacific on the Islands of Bikini and Einewetok. I recall viewing this horror just before heading off to high school.

In March of 1948, I joined an aviation club in seventh grade, which was directed by Mr. McCabe, a teacher who was a U.S. Navy pilot during World War II. He was quite an interesting man who flew Grumman F4F's and F6F's off an aircraft carrier in the Pacific. Mr. McCabe organized a field trip to LaGuardia Airport, which was twelve miles north of P.S.155 in South Ozone Park, Queens, NY. We arrived at school at 08:00 and departed for La Garbage (LaGuardia) at 09:00 in a yellow school bus. It was raining quite heavily when we arrived at the Marine Air Terminal at 09:35. We toured the old terminal that had a mural commissioned during the WPA (Works Project Administration) of the 1930's, entitled "Flight" which was the story of man's quest to fly. It is still in existence today.

The commercial aircraft in existence, at that time, was the Douglas DC3, DC4, Convair 240, Martin 404, and possibly the DC6. As I stated earlier, LaGuardia was all filled land and through the years had been settling steadily, which requires an extensive system of gigantic pumps and dikes to stem the tide from Bowery Bay. This is similar to the situation found in Holland and New Orleans. These pumps are still in existence. I will *cut to the chase.*

On a rainy day in March of 1948, apparently, the dike system failed, the pump system was unable to relieve the amount of water emptying onto the tarmac at LaGuardia from Bowery Bay and the torrential rainfall. The airport became flooded and consequently, was closed to aircraft movements. Mr. McCabe was a man who operated quite well under stressful situations based on his military background during WWII.

We students were restricted to viewing aircraft in the six hangars at the airport; everything else was shut down, as there was no electrical power on the airport, rendering the water pumping system inoperative. Mr. McCabe, our fearless leader and teacher kept his cool during these trying times. His opening statement was, "Here's the story, guys." We finally went back to our yellow school bus, ate our lunch and returned to our grade school. I found his course to be very interesting for the remainder of the year.

We had another trip, this time to Idlewild; when this airport was still in its infancy, with very limited facilities at that time. I joined another club, known as Youth Builder's Club, hosted by a really refined lady Miss Klaus on whom I developed an instant childish crush. Miss Klaus will reappear later on in my *"quest for flight."*

I attended P.S. 155 until graduation on June 24,1949. On the afternoon of my graduation, I had to take a battery of tests at John Adams High School, my new high school, situated adjacent to Aqueduct Race Track. During the racing season, we listened to the on-track announcer and would bet our lunch money on the races. Included in my quest for knowledge as a high school student, I learned how to handicap the races with proficiency. This can only happen in New York City and sounds like a scene from Guy and Dolls. Another thing that influenced my life then and now, which I received from my father, was a love for music and the saxophone. Can you visualize a four-foot-two inch tall, 90-pound skinny kid lugging a C melody saxophone in a forty-inch case for a distance of three miles from home to school for lessons? I played in the school band in grade school and in high school.

Chapter Four:

My High School Days,
September 03, 1949 to June 24, 1953

I started my high school education on September 03, 1949. Since my father never held a steady job and I lacked the guidance from a concerned family, I had no direction of where to go or what subjects to take. The only positive influences that made an impression on me came from my Uncle Tom, who influenced me later in life to join the US Navy and my Uncle Charley who influenced me in becoming a pilot.

I was a skinny little kid; therefore, sports were out as a profession. My father did influence me in music, and his perfectionism influenced me greatly. These traits showed themselves in the building trades; woodworking, painting, plumbing, electricity, wallpapering, drafting and electronics, to name a few. These skills became a major part of my life and are still with me today. I can repair almost anything.

During my four years in high school I played in the band. I became very interested in science, which consisted of earth science, biology, and chemistry. I loved history and music theory. As far as sports went, I played baseball, handball, swam and ran track. One thing I really enjoyed was playing "stick ball." For those who did not grow up on the streets of a major city, this consisted of "fast pitching," which was accomplished in a schoolyard against a handball court wall. A rectangular box was inscribed on the wall in chalk, to depict a strike zone. The bat consisted of a 40-inch long broom handle. The ball was made of pink rubber, manufactured by a corporation known as Spaulding, aka, "Spaldeen" in Brooklyneeze.

In the other form of "stick ball," the ball was slow pitched and you hit the ball on a bounce. It was played on a city street that was the width of a city block with two automobiles, one on each side of the street; the length of the "field" consisted of four sewer grates that were approximately 100 feet apart. The teams consisted of the men from the neighborhood and included our fathers, neighbors, and visitors. We would challenge other blocks and would play for the championship of the neighborhood.

Some of my neighbors were the Casey brothers, Harold and Slim, who were in their twenties and a man who was quite influential in my life, Steve Buskey, an iron-worker. Steve lived across the street in an apartment with his wife, Margie; they had a daughter Peggy and a son, Steve. The father was ten years older than me and was in the Army Air Corps during WWII. He was a great guy and grew up on the streets of Manhattan in, "Hell's Kitchen." He helped me with my baseball. He also helped me in many ways especially in explaining "the facts of life." During those days after the war, no one had an air-conditioned apartment. We would sit on the brick staircase on the front of the house known as a "stoop."

As a young teenager I was selected at times to play Pinochle with the men. This was a disaster because I could not count cards. I still cannot count cards today. My father would become very angry with this. It was frustrating to him but I was just a thirteen-year-old kid and doing the best I could.

Living in a city neighborhood that was quite compact, you had to learn to get along with everyone else. This was not the case regarding one of our neighbors who lived two houses away from us. He was a bachelor, a mama's boy, who lived with his elderly parents. His only possessions were his bulldog and his Sherlock Holmes pipe. He would chase us kids and threaten us with bodily harm. We would throw firecrackers in his flowerbeds and blow them up. We were devils! We gave him the name "bull dog face" when he scowled, he resembled his mutt. My father punched his lights out when he complained about our band rehearsal… a big mistake.

I subconsciously decided that I wanted to explore a career in aviation and noted it in my high school yearbook. It was customary to let the world *out there* know what profession you would seek, or where you would attend college, or what military branch of service you would enter. I did not intend to go to college; it never entered into the equation. I had mediocre grades, no guidance, and no financial aid to seek *"The Impossible Dream."* I decided, and wrote at the bottom of my photo, that I would explore the Academy of Aeronautics, an aviation mechanics trade school at LaGuardia Airport. Why I inserted that, to this day, I still do not know; however, it was my first step in the right direction toward an unknown career.

I graduated from high school on June 24, 1953, decided to take the summer off and hang out at Rockaway Beach and 108th Street, during the birth of **Rock and Roll**. Incidentally, I graduated a year early thanks to a rapid advance program; thus, I was seventeen years old on May 25th and graduated one month later. During my teenage life, my mother was quite over protective of her only son. This was a typical Italian mother thing. Therefore, I was not permitted to go to the beach without adult supervision. She even gave me a hard time after I graduated from high school. I did not drive a car; in fact, I did not receive a driver's license until I was discharged from the U.S. Navy at age 21. Kids have it made today! I had to take out a loan to purchase a car after my military service to learn how to drive. In retrospect, throughout my life, I always had to accomplish things the hard way; nothing came easily. We did not have an automobile because of the expense and public transportation was quite plentiful. The beach scene was great; I hung around with a bunch of musicians, one of who is Professor Leo Ursini at Columbia University who played with the Frank Sinatra Organization.

One other musician who deserves honorable mention is a trombonist named Larry O'Brien, the leader of the Glenn Miller Orchestra. I first met Larry at a high school band rehearsal in September of 1949. He was a long lanky kid with a trombone in his hand; resembling Glenn Miller sans spectacles... he had a temporary pronounced indentation in his lips from the mouthpiece. To this day, whenever the orchestra comes to our neck of the woods, Larry, John Nickerson, who sat next to Larry in the trombone section and I get together for a family reunion. Larry always makes it a point to acknowledge John Adams High School and us. He's a great guy and an outstanding musician. Go to one of his concerts and mention my name. He does a superb job with these young musicians.

After the summer of '53 passed, I decided that it was high time to support myself by seeking employment.

Chapter Five:

Betwixt, Between,
June 25, 1953 to January 17, 1955

I n September of 1953, I secured a "no-brainer" type of job as a messenger with the Port of New York Authority (PONYA) at 111 8th Avenue, NY. My duties were to pick up and deliver inter-office mail, serve coffee to the executives and commissioners and perform numerous other menial tasks, as they saw fit. I earned $40.00 per week. I still had no idea of where I was going or what profession I would seek for the rest of my life. I worked in the mailroom for P&AS (Purchase and Administrative Services) Department. We wore gray coats with a badge and a number and resembled busboys at a restaurant. It was our job to pick up, sort and deliver inter-office mail. It gave us the opportunity to converse and fall in love with the young and beautiful secretaries fresh out of high school and college, who were making more money than we were. I enjoyed visiting the Aviation Development Department, responsible for designing New York International Airport. The Director of the department was a gentleman named Thomas M. Sullivan. Mr. Sullivan would re-enter my life some years later as the designer of the Dallas Fort Worth Airport.

Just across the street was a hole in the wall Jewish delicatessen named Ben's Deli. Their menu consisted of all kosher and freshly cooked turkey, pastrami, corned beef and assorted cold cut sandwiches, too numerous to mention. Incidentally, they even had freshly cooked hams, which is a no-no, if you are Jewish. They also sold matzo balls, blintzes and various other Jewish delicacies, delivered and served coffee to the executives at

111 Eighth Avenue, New York, NY. At times we patronized a chain called "Martin's Bar." For two dollars, you could get a sandwich and a beer for lunch. We'd go to a park on sixteenth-street and play basketball or handball. This neighborhood was predominantly Hispanic which was probably featured in the film "West Side Story" for the Jets and Shark's "Rumble." At Christmas time, the offices closed and every department within the building held its annual Christmas party, including the many tenants. The entire building shut down early and each department held its own party on the same day. It was the custom that any employee was welcome at every department's festivities. The messengers were the main attraction of all the parties... we were the young and the restless and loved to dance. On the other hand, the executives were there for other reasons. I will let you draw your own conclusions. Everyone got a little "Shifaced," but all had a good time. The executives were not happy with us lowly messengers. On one occasion, on my way home by subway, I fell asleep and wound up at the terminus of that particular subway system.... you snooze you lose.

The Port Authority Building occupied an entire New York City block, from Eighth Avenue to Ninth Avenue from Fifteenth Street to Sixteenth Street and was fifteen stories high. The building had elevators that could elevate an eighteen-wheeler tractor-trailer. On our lunch breaks we headed down to Greenwich Village, sat in the park and viewed the scenery, the area adjacent just southwest of Fourteenth Street encompassing West Forth Street.

In January of 1954 and early on a Saturday morning, normally a day of rest... I received an urgent telephone call from my department head at the Port of New York Authority that I report to work ASAP. When I reported an hour and a half later, I was instructed to deliver to every major newspaper in the New York and New Jersey area, a press release formulated by Ms. Lee K. Jaffe, Director of the Public Relations Department of the Port of New York Authority. It was a statement issued by Mr. Austin J. Tobin, Executive Director of The Port Authority, pertaining to the fact that TV and Radio star Arthur Godfrey, a pilot of a DC3, buzzed the air traffic control tower at Teterboro, New Jersey. According to Mr. Personality, he was making a crosswind correction on takeoff and just happened to come into close proximity to the control tower. After some research, I discovered that Mr. Godfrey requested to utilize another runway for takeoff and the control tower disapproved his request. It became a clear case of "He said, she said." In the final analysis, Mr. Godfrey received a six-month suspension of his pilot's license. Incidentally, the reason that the Port Authority got involved was that the PA owned the Teterboro Airport.

On a lunch break on September 25, 1954, I took a trip up to Times Square, to the US Armed Forces Recruiting Station, which I am sure that you have seen in many movies and joined the U.S. Navy. The Navy offered more specialized aviation rates for an enlisted man than the Air Force. I requested a rate associated with naval aviation and I stated that I did not want to be inducted into the Navy until after January 1, 1955.

Sometime in October of 1954 in New York City as a messenger for the Port Authority, I had to make a delivery to Lexington Avenue and the famous Fifty-Second Street, noted for its jazz clubs and also the world-renowned 21 Club at 21 West 52nd Street. As I approached the corner of Lex and 52nd (New York slang), there were all kinds of commotion and equipment focused on a subway grating over the Lexington Avenue subway station for the IND subway system. I discovered that it was a film crew in the process of shooting the world famous scene with Marilyn Monroe's dress being blown over her head by a passing train below ground. In actuality it was not the train that blew up her dress, it was a strategically placed high- powered fan below ground. The first time I saw Marilyn Monroe in the movies was in *"Some Like It Hot"* with Jack Lemmon and Tony Curtis. I hung around for the shooting of this scene, and instantly fell in love then and there, and continue to be partial to blondes to this day. My present girlfriend's name is Marilynn from Brooklyn, with two n's and she is a blonde with very short hair. When I returned to my office, I got chewed out for being quite late, I lied, said that I became quite ill and had to sit down and rest, when in reality, I was simply and forever smitten with a malady known as "Marilynitis," in honor of this blonde goddess.

Chapter Six:

The Birth and Development of My Aviation Career in the Military January 18, 1955 to February 21, 1957

I spent the holidays at home and was inducted into the US Navy on January 18 1955. Unbeknownst to me at that time, I just guaranteed my life's ambition as a pilot. We were sworn in at 39 Whitehall Street in Manhattan, loaded on busses and shipped to Bainbridge, MD for eight weeks of basic training. I was a skinny kid of about 102 pounds; how I passed the physical with mononucleosis, I will never know. Naturally, you start your new found career with a crew cut, which automatically makes you all look like prisoners of war. We received our physical examination and a series of shots that virtually took us to our knees.

We were assigned to Company 5533 with chief petty officer, George Dudley as our company commander. Every morning we woke up to O Maryland, My Maryland, otherwise known as, Old Tannenbaum, my Tannenbaum. We were all from the NY and NJ area except for Edward Hall who was from Newport News, VA or as he would say "Noo put News," VA. Another guy was a little southern gentleman named Shorty Byrum from the hills of Kentucky. Please don't ask me from where; I never heard of the joint. Edward Hall became the company leader. Shorty Byrum who was about five-feet-two inches tall and resembled Lou Costello, he carried his rifle exactly the way Lou Costello did in the army movie, "Buck Privates," which was made in the 40s.

I wound up in sickbay with a relapse of mononucleosis; however, it occurred on a weekend and with massive doses of anti-biotic, I was able to attend school on Monday.

I had it made in boot camp; I played clarinet in the first regiment band, which excluded me from drilling with the rest of the company. It also relieved me from service week, which consisted of mess cooking or latrine duty. When the rest of the company did this, I would go to the music room and rehearse. We got to play every morning for colors, which entailed saluting the American Flag, and playing the Star Spangled Banner, Anchors Away and Sousa marches. One snowy morning in February, the band was traveling between regiments to play for colors at an adjoining regiment. It was customary for the snare drummer to give the marching band rim taps on the side of his drum while marching, so that we would keep in step. We were traveling along to the cadence of the rim taps. All of a sudden, we heard a crash and we saw the snare drummer rolling down the side of the embankment with the snare drum wrapped around his head, ending up in a snow bank. The snare drummer did not see the fire hydrant as he approached and subsequently crashed into it, causing all hell to break loose. It took us about fifteen minutes to gain our composure.

We got extra liberty for playing at "smokers" or intramural fights. In my company there was a recruit named Freeman Favors who played in the drum and bugle corps. I mention this at this time, because he entered my life again in the late 1960s.

During the eight weeks of basic training we were tested academically for further schooling and counseling relative to our careers in the Navy. My general classification test (GCT) marks were fairly high. My mechanical aptitude tests scores were quite high; however, my math scores were a little low, which eliminated me from Naval Aviation Cadet Training. Had I known what lay ahead for me, I would have prepped for the exam; this is the norm today. My interest in Naval Aviation and my test results helped me to receive schooling at the Naval Aviation Preparatory School in Norman, OK and finally Navy Aerographer's Mate (Naval Aerology/Meteorology) "A" School in Lakehurst, NJ. It was while I was traveling from Norman, OK to Lakehurst, NJ that I received my first airplane ride from Oklahoma City to Philadelphia with a fuel stop in Evansville, IN. The aircraft was a Super Douglas DC3, which carried thirty-two passengers as opposed to the Standard DC3. The charter was by General Airlines, *The Route of The Roses* out of Portland, OR, which eventually merged into Western Airlines.

I am sure you recognize the name of Lakehurst, NJ, the home of the US Navy lighter than aircraft known as the "Blimp." It was the scene of the horrific explosion of the German Airship Hindenburg in 1937. Incidentally, there is a memorial placed at the crash site. We had a beautiful female WAVE named Mary Lou McKee in our class. We were assigned as a team to track a PIBAL (pilot balloon) together with an instrument known as a theodolite, which is similar to a surveyor's transit; however, it measures azimuth and elevation in degrees. Every minute on a stopwatch, we had to record the azimuth and elevation of the balloon until it burst, then plot it on a chart, which gave us altitude and associated wind direction and velocity. On one occasion, I was operating the theodolite and Mary Lou was recording the coordinates. She was standing behind me looking over my left shoulder, wearing a most provocative perfume. Incidentally, I am a sucker for a sexy blonde wearing delicate fragrance even to this day, especially gardenias. It distracted me so totally that I lost my cool, the balloon and had to terminate the tracking. I wonder how it is in today's military with the amount of women in uniform?

I recall another incident that was quite hilarious. It involved Mary Lou once again. This time it was in class and pertained to instruction in weather observations onboard a ship at sea, known as shipboard code. Shipboard code was the recording of weather data pertaining to the state of the sea, direction of the ship, etc. This data is published on a weather map and consists of additional data, different from the regular data associated with a land station.

This data consisted of the condition of the ocean at the time of the observation, which included the height of the waves, the direction of the swells and the interval between the swells. Our instructor for this segment was a first class petty officer, which looked and spoke like Mr. Peepers, known better as Wally Cox, and was a first class nerd. This poor instructor turned bright red when he had to explain to us Navy men and Ms. Mary Lou McKee, the WAVE, the one portion of the shipboard code entitled, "The Period of The Wave." Mary Lou was a sharp lady and took it in stride.

During training at Lakehurst, we were required to march to lunch as a class. This one fine July day, we were marching to chow alongside the tennis courts when we were distracted by a blimp wandering aimlessly, obviously out of control, heading straight for us. We scattered, watched the blimp crash through the tennis court fence and proceed north. It appears that the U.S. Navy was taking acceptance of the blimp from Goodyear, the manufacturer; on board were Navy personnel and Goodyear representatives. Blimps are very difficult to land in windy conditions due to their enormous size. As the blimp was positioning for a landing, it was hit by a gust of wind that caused it to pitch violently to one side, thus separating one of the two reciprocating piston engines from the gondola. Because of the confusion and lack of communications in the gondola, everyone left the premises except two people. One individual was releasing helium, so that the blimp would settle to the surface, while the other individual was jettisoning sand bags, which were being used as a ballast, to make the airship lighter, in order for it to keep flying. In the end the blimp reached an altitude at which it would neither climb nor descend. This occurred over a farmer's field with Navy helicopters buzzing around the blimp like bees. There was even talk of shooting it down. Finally, the personnel on board were able to relieve the blimp of its helium, allowing it to settle into the farmer's field. Naturally, a lawsuit ensued.

After class and prior to going to dinner, we headed to the TV room in the barracks to view a new local show from WFIL channel 6 from nearby Philadelphia, named "American Bandstand," with an unknown emcee named Dick Clark. We would watch these dudes dance with these sharp looking chicks while we were in this stinking barracks in the boondocks of New Joisey with nothing to do but drool. We decided to send away for some tickets and were hopeful we'd get on the show. We finally got four tickets and we went to the live show on a Friday afternoon after class. We danced with some of those beautiful ladies who would eventually dance on American Bandstand when it became nationally syndicated. This was in July of 1955 and I was nineteen years old. I fell in love; I think her name was Darlene. While attending the show we danced to a group called "Rocco and the Saints," which consisted of a handsome trumpet player named Frankie Avalone, who became the teen idol named Frankie Avalon. He starred in those beach party movies of the 1960's. There was also a drummer named Bobby Ridarelli, later known as Bobby Rydell, the singer and a great comedian. It seems that Frankie and Bobby came from an Italian neighborhood in South Philadelphia. Bobby imitated an Old Italian gentleman named Mr. Limo who came from the old country. Bobby's rendition of Mr. Limo's Italian accent and feebleness of old age had us rolling in the aisles. The day that we were there, they featured a male guest star named Walden Robert Cassotto, who later changed his name to Bobby Darin. I discovered that Bobby Darin was born May 14, 1936 and I was born May 25, 1936. Unfortunately, Bobby Darin died at age 37... he was such a great entertainer. Frankie Avalon, Bobby Rydell and Fabian are still on the road, recreating their Rock and Roll hits of the 1950's. Don't miss them; they put on a great show.

Upon completion of Aerology School, Bob Briones, a fellow New Yorker from Queens and I were assigned to NAAS (Naval Auxiliary Air Station) Corry Field, Pensacola FL, a great duty station under the command of Lieutenant Robert W. Lindeloff from McKeesport, PA, who acquired the nickname, Mr. Winds Aloft, quite apropos. We were assigned to the flight operations duty section, a zero duty section, which meant that when we weren't standing a watch, we were free to go off base until our next watch. We slept in a special wing of the barracks since we worked around the clock and were required to sleep during the day. It was there at Corry Field that my love for aviation truly came to life.

I was entitled to flight pay because I had to be qualified to take weather observations, not only on the ground but also in the air. I wound up sitting in the back seat of an SNJ, also known as a *slow navy jet*, which is the equivalent to an Air Force T6 North American Texan. I also climbed into the back seat of a T28, North American Trojan; this was and still is a great flying machine equal to some of its WWII predecessors. I had many dreams of becoming a U.S. Navy Nav Cad and the Top Gun in my class, a la Tom Cruise. Incidentally, two of my first officers who flew for Delta out of Boston with me were "Top Gun" instructors on the Grumman F14. Their names were Vance Walker, who did a walk-on in the first scene and Gregg "Hollywood" Dishart, who did some of the flying in the movie. Gregg said that it was great working with Tom Cruise. Now back to reality, I went cross country on occasions to New York in a T28 or a SNB, *Slow Navy Bomber*, a twin engine, twin tail Beechcraft with an Air Force identifier of a C45. I can also recollect sitting in the back seat of a T28 and proceeding northeast of Atlanta on Green 5, a low frequency airway, with a fuel stop in Spartanburg, SC. We were up about 7,000 feet when the pilot said to me, "there is Stone Mountain" and dummy me asked, "What is that"? Stone Mountain is the southern version of Mount Rushmore. Coming from New York, I never heard of it; however, in years to come, I became very familiar with Stone

Mountain while flying for Delta Air Lines out of Atlanta. During the latter part of my duty at Corry Field, we received a new aircraft known as the Beechcraft T34 Mentor; unfortunately, I never got to ride in this new airplane.

My tour of duty was a wonderful experience for me in many ways. I fell in love twice, once with aviation by being around aircraft every day and then when I met Clarinda Kay Stewart of Roanoke, VA in June of 1956, who had a twin sister named Kim. The relationship did not last however, due to religious, ethnic, and geographical problems. She was a southern belle and I was a New York I-talian. My love for aviation prevailed, thank God. After the day watch, I would sit on the roof of the hangar at Corry Field and watch the Blue Angels, in their Grumman Panthers and eventually Cougars, practicing their maneuvers at main side, NAS Pensacola, Forest Sherman Field, some six miles south of Corry Field.

I have one sad remembrance of Corry Field. One night I was standing in line to see a movie on the base and overheard three aviation cadets discussing their solo flights for the next day in T28s. The three decided they would join up with each other, west of Corry Field and would fly formation over to one of the cadets' father's farm in nearby Southern Alabama. I didn't think much of the rendezvous at that time, but the next day there was a T28 crash in nearby Alabama. The wreckage was placed on the flight operations hangar floor, which is where I worked. I examined the wreckage and discovered that the largest piece was only a yellow three-foot section from the tail, signifying the aircraft "augured in" at a near vertical angle. I also read the accident report and viewed the diagrams of the crash scene. It was the cadet who planned the rendezvous to buzz his father's farm was killed in the crash; the other two did not participate. According to the accident report, the cadet made a low pass of his father's farm and was in a steep, tight climbing left turn, looking back over his right shoulder at his father's farm, not concentrating on his flying. Because of this and his lack of experience, a fatal mistake was made; he inadvertently stalled out due to an excessive angle of attack too close to the ground… he spun in, thus, killing himself. There is an aviation saying, which goes like this, *"There are Old Pilots and there are Bold Pilots; however, there are No Old Bold Pilots."*

While at Corry Field, I became very friendly with two individuals; one was Bill Hoy, an air traffic controller, who had been married to a female Marine who died in an automobile accident. The other was Bruce German, a Navy personnel man who later worked for the United States State Department, as well as, the American Embassy in Iran. He was held hostage from November 04, 1979 to January 20, 1981, a total of 444 days. He was released at the start of Ronald Reagan's Presidential Administration. I really didn't realize this until I saw him deplaning from the aircraft

While in the US Navy, my spare time should have been devoted to my love for aviation and my education; however, I managed to devote a portion of my time to fighting *"the Battle of Pensacola Bay…"* chasing young southern ladies up and down Pensacola Beach. I also became a floor boy at a local roller rink. What did you expect a nineteen-year-old with an over abundance of Testosterone to do so far away from home?

I was assigned to flight operations and it was our duty to collect pertinent weather data for all flight operations in and out of the Pensacola area. Our department briefed the pilots on all significant weather associated with their route of flight. This would become very valuable to me during my tenure with the airlines as a pilot. One of the perks working in flight operations was that we had the information on all cross country flights and their destinations. I got free "hops" to New York's Floyd Bennett Field or to Richmond, VA to see my girl friend in Roanoke. On one occasion, there was a hop available to NAS New York's Floyd Bennett Field in an SNB Navy Serial Number Navy 29636. It was scheduled to leave on a Friday afternoon and return Sunday evening. The flight was under the command of Lieutenant Commander William Reilly, assisted by Lieutenant Roger Smith. If approved, it would consist of Tony Diers, aviation machinist mate first class and me, as passengers. We left Corry Field, Pensacola, FL at 16:00 on an IFR (instrument flight rules) flight plan with a stop in Richmond, VA for fuel, then continued on to NAS New York aka, Floyd Bennett Field. We flew a low frequency airway known as Green 5, which for our flight plan terminated at Idlewild Airport in New York. We then were to proceed to NAS New York Airport via VFR (visual flight rules). When we arrived over Idlewild, we were cleared to proceed via the flight-planned route to NAS New York, which was direct. Both pilots were not familiar with the route; I suggested that they make a left turn and proceed southwest via the Belt Parkway and when they saw the Marine Parkway Bridge, the airport would be to the left of the bridge. This procedure is known as *local knowledge,* coupled with situation awareness, which is to know where you are at all times. These became valuable tools during my thirty-and one-half years as an airline pilot. I'll elaborate on these procedures in subsequent chapters.

We arrived at NAS New York at midnight and my parents were there to greet me. I spent Saturday with my family and had to leave early Sunday morning for a 08:00 departure. The weather was quite foggy and the ceiling and visibility were right at *minimums,* which were a 200-foot ceiling and one-half mile visibility. The crew inspected the aircraft and we departed southwest toward the Marine Parkway Bridge, which connected the mainland to the barrier island known as "The Rockaways." Upon entering the clouds shortly after takeoff, the aircraft pitched up and then pitched down violently and banked to the left. We had entered into a stall. The crew recovered and we broke out of the clouds once more at about two hundred feet above the ground. We came very close to a row of Navy barracks or *buying the farm,* as they say. Upon landing in Richmond VA, we discussed the problem with the crew. Evidently, the ground crew did not install the protective covers over the pitot tubes upon our arrival. These provide ram air pressure to the air speed indicators on the instrument panel. The aforementioned tubes were heated, however, from being exposed to the elements, some water had accumulated in the tubes and caused some erroneous readings. The pilots did a superb job; otherwise, I would not be here today to tell you this story. It was a great learning experience for me and it became invaluable in the years to come. Everything that I learned and did during my career in aviation gave me an enormous advantage over my military counterparts. Their training was much more regimented than mine; however, I had the common sense and a great deal more of practical knowledge. I also learned from other people's mistakes. These advantages ultimately helped me immensely.

Eventually, all good things come to an end; as did my stay in Pensacola. Unfortunately, both of my parents became ill, which necessitated me leaving the U.S. Navy to return home and support them and my two younger sisters. I was sad and heavy of heart, but I had to do what was best for my family. I received my hardship discharge on February 21, 1957 and arrived home that same day via National Airlines to Jacksonville and then on to LaGuardia.

Chapter Seven:

My Return to the Port of New York Authority, February 22, 1957 to June 09, 1957

I returned to my clerical aide position at the Port of New York Authority in New York City and was assigned to the Purchase and Administration Services Department, under Mr. James Clarke McGuire, in the duplication section, which was basically a print shop. This was no challenge for me and I was bored as hell; however, the training that I received then was quite invaluable in formulating this manuscript. I traveled by bus and subway to 14th Street and 8th Avenue in Manhattan every morning. One Saturday, I had to work and a group of us were called in to view a new promotional movie of the Port of New York and New Jersey. This was the brainchild of J.C. McGuire and consisted of a typical day at the Port of NY & NJ. The opening scene was of the Statue of Liberty at sunset looking at Lower Manhattan from seaward, with a view of a buoy in the foreground clanging its bell. It had some wonderful music specifically composed with some soothing nautical reflections within its score. The movie was approximately one hour and forty-five minutes long. It showed the facilities of the port, the airports, the tunnels, and the bridges. I do not know how much it cost to produce this project, however, it was modified thanks to a new musical instrumental composition that came on the market entitled, "Ebb Tide," played by Frank Chacksfield and his orchestra that, excuse the expression, *blew their presentation right out of the water.*

Another highlight of my association with the Port of NY Authority was to hand deliver a personal letter from the executive director of the

Port Authority, Mr. Austin J. Tobin, to the Governor of New York, the Honorable Robert F. Wagner via the New York Central Railroad traveling up the Hudson River.

While working in the Duplication Section for the Port of NY Authority, I worked with a gentleman named Al Neidermeyer. This name re-entered my life in 2006 while viewing the movie entitled "World Trade Center," staring Nicholas Cage... the story of two Port Authority police officers who risked their lives to save trapped victims of the World Trade Center destruction on September 11, 2001 caused by Terrorists. At the conclusion of the movie, there was a list of the Port Authority personnel who perished and the name Alphonse Neidermeyer III appeared. I have an uncanny memory. I experienced a flashback from 2006 to 1957... some thirty-nine years... and I lost my composure. I discovered through research that the individual who perished was the forty-year-old son of my friend and co-worker. He was a policeman at the World Trade Center and died trying to save others. As the saying goes, *there is no greater love than for the one who lays down his life for a friend.*

God Bless Them All, Requiescat In Pace, Latin (Rest in Peace).

One other adventure at the Port Authority, which comes to mind, was that the P&AS Department had a division that constructed models of the airports, bridges, tunnels, etc. There was a model to be delivered to Mitchell Air Force Base in Hempstead, Long Island, NY and the driver Harry Andrews, who was from New Jersey, did not know how to get there. Being familiar with the area, I offered to write down the directions; but Harry suggested that I go with him, which I did. It gave me a chance to see some of the latest Air Force aircraft. Mitchell Field was the base for the 514th Troop Carrier Wing, which utilized the KC-119, twin engine, twin tail troop transports, known as "The Flying Box Car," or as author Chuck Lunsford called it, a Packet Fairchild. I got to ride in one of these at a later date with the Civil Air Patrol. It was summer in New York City and I was getting restless. I started to miss my U.S. Navy life and the excitement of being around aviation, so I decided to go to the U.S. Weather Service at JFK and seek employment as a weather observer. This was similar to what I did in the U.S. Navy, but without a college degree in meteorology, there was little I could do career wise.

A defining moment in my life occurred when I enlisted into the U.S. Navy on January 18, 1955 and, unbeknownst to me, the GI Bill of Rights associated with the Korean Conflict was terminated on January 31, 1955. I did not participate in the Korean Conflict, but I was entitled to receive benefits under the GI Bill, which turned out to be my salvation.

While still employed with the Port of NY Authority, I participated in a three-day battery of tests and evaluations under the auspices of the New York State Employment Service in Long Island City, Queens, NY. After the tests and evaluation, it was determined that I had the knowledge and potential to be an aircraft mechanic or some position associated with aviation operations. Living close to Idlewild Airport, I decided to visit Aviation Enterprises, an employment agency in Jamaica, Queens, specializing in airline employment. The agency scheduled me for an interview with Mr. Walter Peto, Station Manager for Northeast Airlines at LaGuardia Airport and also his assistant, Carl Smitelli. I was interviewed extensively. If I wanted the position, I would have to start as a passenger service agent, also known as a ramp rat at $62.50 a week. The first I heard of Northeast Airlines was on February 01, 1957 when a leased Flying Tigers DC6A took off on runway 04 at LaGuardia and crashed on Riker's Island, situated just northeast of the airport. There were 20 fatalities out of a total of 101 souls on board. The probable cause was, according to the NTSB, " the failure of the captain to: 1) properly observe and interpret his flight instruments, and 2) maintain control of his aircraft." The way I understand the situation was that the aircraft was not properly maintained prior to the lease; however, the aircraft was certified airworthy by the CAA/FAA and I understand that there was quite a bit of corrosion throughout the aircraft, which affected the two independent flight instrument systems on board the aircraft. In my estimation, there had to be some form of instrument problem for that aircraft, which was instructed to maintain runway heading. The runway heading on runway 4 at LaGuardia is 041 degrees magnetic. The aircraft was on a heading of 285 degrees magnetic when it struck Riker's Island, a disparity of 116 degrees left of course. The accident occurred one minute after the start of the takeoff roll. Surely, both pilots would have detected this serious deviation from the runway heading. The captain became director of flight control and was my boss when I worked in flight control. He was a kind, gentle person who was quite aristocratic.

Chapter Eight:

Airline Life on the Ground and Flight Training, June 10, 1957 to February 23, 1963

I accepted the position with Northeast Airlines at New York's LaGuardia Airport on June 10, 1957. It entailed shift work and working weekends. It was a foot in the door. Northeast Airlines, at that time, utilized the DC3, Convair 240s and was receiving ten new DC6Bs for their Miami route. While working late at LaGuardia and also Idlewild/JFK, one would occasionally hear a comedian on the airport public address system make some off-color announcements. Two come to mind; one was, "Will Albert Anastasia kindly report to the barber shop? You have a visitor." FYI, the Mafia gunned down Albert Anastasia on October 25, 1957 at the Park Central hotel barbershop in Manhattan. The other one that I remember was, "Will Miss Carriage kindly report to the airport medical facility." Cute, but dumb.

Equipment and procedures were in the dark ages then compared with today; however, it all contributed to a highly valuable learning process. I've done some research on airliners and offer some tidbits of trivia that just might come in handy someday. The Douglas DC3 was manufactured in 1935, the DC4 in 1939, the DC6 in 1946, the DC7 in 1953, the DC8 in 1958, the DC9 in 1965 and the DC10 in 1971. The Boeing 707 was manufactured in 1957, Boeing 727 in 1963, B737 in 1966, Boeing 747 in 1969, Boeing 757 in 1982, the Boeing 767 in 1981 and the Boeing 777 in 1994.

After a few months, I was promoted to an operations agent, responsible for preparing flight plans, printing weather reports, performing weight and balance calculations, and the distribution of cargo on flights and associations with the flight crews, which was similar to my duties in the US Navy. Throughout my ground career with NE, I worked positions at LGA and IDL. In 1958, due to an expansion of the DC6B service to Florida, Northeast Airlines constructed a makeshift terminal at the Marine Air Terminal at LaGuardia. It was built of two by fours and plywood. This was done to relieve the main terminal congestion of the Miami traffic. The DC6B carried seventy-six passengers and with the new service, invariably, the flights would be oversold. So what's new?

I had the opportunity of working at the ground operations shack one snowy Sunday afternoon in February at the Marine Air Terminal facility at LaGuardia. Things were quiet and everyone took a lunch break, which meant that I was by myself. We were not too far from the run-up pad for the departures on runway 04; during the piston engine days, it was a requirement to run-up each engine to about 1500 revolutions per minute, so that you could check each magneto for a minimal drop, signifying the individual spark plug for that cylinder on that engine was receiving ignition correctly. Incidentally, there were two individual spark plugs per cylinder and two magnetos per engine. I would listen to the run-ups and wouldn't think anything of it; it was music to ears. On that particular day, as I was performing the menial tasks associated with ground operations, I was distracted by the constant revving up of both engines of an aircraft on the adjoining ramp. The engines advanced and retarded. It became so disconcerting I decided to see what the problem was. Upon exiting the office, I discovered a Lockheed Loadstar, which was a twin tailed, twin-engine corporate aircraft, causing the disturbance. I approached from the left side (FYI: one always approaches an aircraft from the left side… that's where the pilot in command is seated). The sliding glass side window opened and a beautiful middle aged woman motioned to me to get on the radio. I telephoned Butler Aviation, the tenant next to Northeast Airlines, to send a crew out to park and service her aircraft. After the aircraft was parked and secured, the beautiful woman came over to me and personally thanked me for my assistance. I recognized her immediately... it was Jackie Cochran, as famous an aviatrix as Amelia Earhart.

During Northeast Airlines' entrance into the Miami market, we had a sportscaster from Miami, named Jim Dooley doing commercials on radio and TV yelling "Come on Down!" This advertisement campaign in New York resulted in quite a few little elderly Jewish ladies traveling to and from South Beach and Collins Avenue in Miami. One morning, one such lady approached passenger service supervisor, Millie Twomey. The woman was in tears; she had a fear of flying. The Jewish lady had a real thick Yiddish accent making it difficult for Millie to understand her. In an attempt to calm the woman, Millie mentioned that the DC6B in which she would be flying to Miami was brand new and had a very experienced crew. Millie also told the lady that the pilots were million-mile accident-free pilots and that they would do everything within their power to guarantee that she would be well taken care of. To assure the Jewish lady even further, Millie mentioned that on her flight today there would be a very famous person on board; she would be traveling with Billy Graham. The elderly Jewish lady seemed mystified and exclaimed in a thick Yiddish accent, "So, Who's Billy Graham?"

While working at the Marine Terminal for Northeast Airlines, we were required to prepare and service for flight a Convair 240 with an aircraft number of N240K, the "Caroline," in honor of Senator John F. Kennedy's young daughter. This aircraft was the personal aircraft of the Kennedy family of Hyannis port, MA and became the aircraft used by Senator John F. Kennedy during his race for the White House in 1960. I came in personal contact with Senator John Kennedy on numerous occasions. I was quite impressed with him and his personality, plus his concern for the common people. The senator was always kind and personable and was a genuine individual. His wife, Jackie, was quite refined and elegant; she became one of the finest First Ladies of the twentieth century, including Nancy Reagan at the top of my list. Presidents and First Ladies should try to emulate this refined couple from "Camelot," to a degree.

In 1958, I was working ground operations at Idlewild, when one of our new DC6B's left the gate for Miami... it was flight 631. Upon departure, everyone went to lunch, including maintenance. I had to close out the paperwork on the flight and send the weight and balance data to Miami, which consisted of the distribution of the cargo and baggage on the associated flight. As I was finishing up the paperwork I received a telephone call from Port Authority Operations that the flight to Miami had just received a "landing gear unsafe" warning light, while taxiing for takeoff; they needed someone to go out with the Port Authority vehicle with a set of landing gear safety pins and insert them in the landing gear, so that the aircraft could safely taxi back to the gate for maintenance, without the fear of the landing gear collapsing. As the only one available, I went to the maintenance shack, picked up a set of three pins, two for the main gear and one for the nose gear. I jumped into the yellow Port Authority car and sped down the taxiway to the apron surrounding the departure end of runway 22R. I assumed that the Port Authority vehicle was in contact with ground control and the aircraft and had advised everyone concerned that I would be under the aircraft, inserting the pins. I had seen this done quite often when an aircraft came to the gate, but this would be the first time for me, so I was quite scared and cautious. I approached the aircraft from the aft, being careful to stay under the belly of the aircraft and away from the gigantic propellers. In preparation for the insertion of the landing gear pin, I held on to the main gear strut. I gingerly inserted the associated landing gear safety pin into the left main gear, which was quite close to the left inboard engine. I then proceeded under the belly of the aircraft to the right main gear and repeated the same process. During this procedure, so far, I was quite proud of myself. I then cautiously and slowly worked my way forward under the gleaming aluminum belly to the nose gear, making sure that I was no way near the rotating propellers. During this period of time, I was not visible to the flight crew and assumed the operator in the Port Authority vehicle was keeping the ground controller and the flight crew aware of my progress. I am only 5'7" tall, so I was unable to reach the hole in the landing gear strut for the nose gear pin. I had to climb up on the nose wheel tire and insert the foot long pin made of stainless steel through a hole specifically provided, so that the nose gear would not collapse, While on the tire and inserting the pin, the aircraft nose gear strut was compressing and extending due to the thrust from all four of the Pratt and Whitney R-2800 engines that were at idle at about 1000 revolutions per minute; however, there was enough thrust being developed to simulate a ride on a bucking bronco. It really had me quite shaken up. To cut to the chase, I completed my assigned task, walked up to the front of the aircraft to give the crew the customary thumbs up, signifying that the pins were in place. I looked up and saw the first officer, Bob Therrian, with his body hanging out the window on the right side, searching as if to see if there was anyone under the aircraft. I discovered later that no one advised the crew I would be inserting the pins. This severe case of a lack of communications could have cost me my life.

Northeast Airlines, as every other airline on this planet had certain colorful pilots who will be remembered for eternity. One such individual was known as, "Chrome Dome, the Gadget Man". He was a balding captain on the DC6B and eventually, the B727. The shiny headed one lived in Epping, NH but flew out of New York. He traveled with certain accoutrements that he kept neatly placed in his oversized black flight bag, which included a neatly cleaned and pressed white silk scarf, two pairs of kid-skinned gloves, one pair of brown leather gloves for everyday flying and one pair of yellow leather gloves for flying under instrument flying conditions. Don't ask… it beats me. Chrome Dome also carried with him a 6 and 5/8s - inch cigarette holder for his favorite Parliament brand filter tipped cigarette. Smoking was permitted on all aircraft at that time. Last, but not least, a neatly pressed white silk handkerchief was placed around the collar of his heavily starched white uniform shirt, to protect the collar from being stained by perspiration. With all this gear in place, it looked like "The Penguin" from Batman was seated in the captain's seat and was ready to take us for an airplane ride. The only thing missing was the top hat and the umbrella. When he, and only he, made the public address system announcements, he called all the stewardesses… are you ready for this? … Trixie and Bubbles!

Another incident that comes to mind involves a Miss Klaus, my former teacher from the seventh grade, who I had mentioned earlier in the book. I was assigned as a passenger service representative supervisor on the midnight to eight shifts in June of 1961. The arrival of a Northeast Convair 880 from Miami was delayed from 22:00 until 00:30. I was the only passenger service agent working the *skeleton crew* shift with some fleet service agents who would unload the baggage and cargo; there were also some mechanics. A very attractive middle-aged woman approached me and stated that her elderly sister was onboard the inbound flight and would require a wheelchair. I suggested she stay with me and that I would accompany her to the base of the ramp. Incidentally, these were the days of zero security. We would carry her down and then accompany the ladies to an awaiting car. There were no jet ways installed back then, so, a ramp was to be pushed up to the aircraft requiring at least two men to position and adjust it to accommodate the aircraft. I secured the help of an additional fleet service agent Don Rhorssen. He was from my neighborhood and had gone to school with my cousin Joey. Upon arrival of the aircraft, I escorted all the passengers off the aircraft first in order not to delay their departure. I would tend to the wheelchair patient next.

With the help of Don, we carried the woman down the ramp in a special conveyance to her waiting wheelchair, taken from the belly of the aircraft. While walking into the terminal and chatting with the two women, subconsciously, I asked the attractive sister, "Are you a teacher?" Why I asked that question, I will never know. Apparently, my subconscious was speaking. The woman looked at me with a total look of surprise. She exclaimed, "Oh my God." I asked, "Were you a teacher at P.S.155 here in Queens?" She answered, "Yes." I asked her name. She replied, "McCullough." I asked her what was her maiden name and she said it was "Klaus." I exclaimed, "You were the teacher of my youth builder's class in 1948." She proceeded to hug and kiss me. She gave me her telephone number and explained that she was retired and living in Greenwich Village. I never called her, but our paths crossed again in 1967 in Boston.

During the five years I was with NE on the ground, I worked every position, including: crew scheduler: senior crew scheduler and assistant flight dispatcher, to name just a few. This experience gave me certain insight and expertise that few other pilots or authors have.

I also served as an assistant flight dispatcher for Northeast Airlines. Northeast Airlines Flight Dispatch Department had just moved from Miami to Hangar Three at IDL/JFK, which is where the first group of hangars were built in the late 1940s. The staff consisted of fourteen CAA/FAA certified dispatchers and four assistant dispatchers, one of whom was little old me. The CAA/FAA licenses Aircraft Dispatchers, whose duties and responsibilities concern the total safety of the individual flights under his or her jurisdiction, and it is shared with the captain of the flight. The dispatchers' duty is the safety of the flight and to notify the pilot of fuel requirements for the particular flight to the destination, holding fuel due to weather or air traffic control, fuel to an alternate, plus an additional forty five minutes for other delays. The weather reports and forecasts for the point of departure, en route weather, destination weather and alternate weather are required, as well as, the particular NOTAM's, (Notice To Airmen). These reports contain navigational outages, if any, other pertinent data, either en route or at airports, here in the states or all over the world. The captain must be kept abreast of any significant changes while en route to his final destination or any other data that may become pertinent. Northeast Airlines Flight Dispatch constructed a flight following board consisting of a time bar that moved on a 24-hour basis. There were flight strips depicting the time en route, the stops associated with the flight, the required reporting points en route and the destination and the posted ETA (estimated time of arrival). This was in the DC6B days, when it took four hours and twenty minutes from New York to Miami.

The Northeast Airlines Aircraft Dispatcher staff consisted of coordinators, dispatchers and assistants plus radio and teletype operators. The coordinators consisted of Fred Weyhrauch, Gerry Swain, Bruce Holloway and Walter Murphy. It was the coordinators' duty to oversee the total operation and make any major decisions pertaining to the everyday operation of the airline. These gentlemen were seasoned veterans who had been with Northeast Airlines since its infancy in the early 1930s. Out of these four, Bruce Holloway stood out in this group, as he was always impeccably dressed, with a white shirt, tie and sport jacket. Bruce was about six foot tall and a little on the portly side and his trademark was a cigar and holder. He gave the impression that he was a sophisticated gentleman of distinction... rightfully so. The aircraft dispatchers were as follows: Jim Begley, Tom Sharkey, Charlie Cleary, Jim Miller, Wes Bacon, Dick Pope, Stan Wolfe, Peter Wong, Freddie Tanzella and Freddie Stuart. I did not know many of these gentlemen personally; it is safe to say that they were WWII veterans. I know for a fact that Jim Begley was a US Navy PBY (Flying Boat) pilot in the South Pacific. It was his job to rescue downed US Navy and Marine pilots who were in harm's way. I understand that Charlie Cleary was a B25 (Mitchell) pilot in the European

Theater of War and flew bombing raids on Germany. The only gentleman I knew fairly well was Stan Wolfe. Stan was a professional drummer, a Kool Kat and he reminded me of a jazz musician from the1950's musical detective program, "Peter Gunn." The music was written by Henry Mancini and had one of the greatest collections of ballads and jazz solos ever recorded. When Stan had some free time or when he was thinking pertaining to a particular flight, Stan would get out two of his neatly sharpened pencils and tap out a complex paradiddle, which consists of a complex exercise in drumming rhythms. The assistant dispatchers were Bernie St. Pierre, Leah Dumas, Dick Calarco and myself. Assistant dispatchers were individuals who would hang in there until a dispatcher position came available, then slide into the slot. This was not the case with Dick Calarco and me. We were there; biding our time… we were aspiring pilots working on our Instrument Ratings with Watson Aviation in Teterboro, NJ and would get hired by a major airline in the early and mid 1960s. All in all, it was great experience and gave us the opportunity to learn the airline industry **"From the Ground Up."**

I would now like to relate two incidents that occurred while I was a crew scheduler in New York. I was called to work in Boston crew scheduling one night, because of an employee's illness. While working the 16:00 to midnight shift in Boston, I was advised that a stewardess did not report in for a flight on a DC3 to Presque Isle, ME, for an overnight. I notified flight control and advised that I would search for a replacement, since it was an hour before the scheduled departure. I also notified the captain of the flight. I will bestow the name "Captain Hostile" upon him. He was a real jerk; I gave him this name, to protect the guilty. I advised flight control and Captain Hostile that I would seek to find a replacement within the next hour. I discovered that there was a flight crew terminating and that the stewardess was "legal" to take the flight to Presque Isle and return the next day. ("Legal" here means that she had not worked too many hours so that even with this added flight she would not be flying more than eight hours in a twenty-four-hour period for the flight requirements.) I notified flight control and the stewardess; problem solved, so I thought. It winds up that Captain Hostile, who lived close to the airport in Winthrop, MA had a girl friend, a stewardess, and left the airport to get her for the flight without notifying anyone, for obvious reasons. In any case, the flight was manned and ready to go; however, there was no captain in sight. I contacted flight control, which was required and explained that the captain had left the airport without authorization and that we would have to take a delay. The coordinator in flight control, Mr. Walter Murphy, instructed me to write it up, which I did. When Captain Hostile arrived with his significant other, I instructed him to get on the flight. The passengers were already on board and so was the young stewardess I had commandeered from the inbound flight. His girlfriend would have to stay home. I also stated that, because of his imprudent actions, he had delayed the flight and that I had to write him up. Captain Hostile was not a happy camper. This person appears in another chapter. Stay tuned for the continuing adventures of Captain Hostile and his escapades.

The other incident is not a pleasant one either. I will not reveal the names with respect for the families. I was working the evening shift in New York crew scheduling on August 15, 1958 and the weather was miserable in the New York and New England area. The area, especially Cape Cod was a solid blanket of fog. Our main aircraft that flew between Boston, New York and Cape Cod was the forty-four passengers Convair 240. The flight schedules consisted of two crews, one from New York and one from Boston, flying opposite each other. These schedules consisted of a series of trips between NY and Boston through Cape Cod, terminating at the pilots' respective domiciles. On this particular evening, the inbound flight from Boston to LaGuardia was quite late and I had to replace the crew for the LaGuardia to Nantucket (ACK) and Boston (BOS) portions of the flight. I assigned another crew that was in between flights at LaGuardia to do the Nantucket and Boston portion in place of the delayed crew and substituted their trip with the delayed inbound crew. The result of this substitution allowed the flight schedule to be maintained with a minimum of delay. Approximately one hour and a half later, we were advised that the crew that I substituted on the LGA to ACK flight had crashed on the approach to ACK and twenty-four of the thirty-five passengers and the crew did not survive. To this day, I still think of my decision and grieve.

During this time period, I became acquainted with many pilots from NE's bases in Boston, New York and Miami. I discovered that I was entitled to benefits under the GI Bill, including flight training. I decided that I would take flight training at Amityville Flight School, Zahn's Airport, Amityville, Long Island, NY, not knowing where it would lead. I arranged it so that I would work the four to twelve shifts and go to flight school in the morning. Zahn's was thirty-five miles east on Long Island.

It was necessary to attend flight school during the early hours of the day and work the night shifts with Northeast Airlines, so that I could fulfill my desire to become an airline pilot. This took a great toll on my personal and social life; no time for girl friends during this period in my life for obvious reasons. While my friends were out partying and dating, I was occupied with working the night or the midnight shift to support my parents and sisters and to pay for my portion of putting myself through flight school. Once again, God Bless the GI Bill. Basically I had no choice. In the years to come, I listened to my pilot associates discuss their careers and the great times they experienced when attending military flight schools and how they frequented their favorite watering holes, such as the famous "Trader John's" in Pensacola, FL. It all made me quite sad because of the experiences and good times I had missed. At that time, there were no approved ground school programs or DVD courses. Therefore, the only way to study for written or flight exams was to read books prepared by the CAA (now FAA). The manuals were one-dimensional training aids, quite limited and lacking. My first flight lesson was on October 17, 1957, with an instructor who will remain nameless, for personal reasons.

During the early days of my flight training at Zahn's, I became an APB, otherwise known as an "airport bum," that consisted of "hangar flying" with other students and instructors. On one occasion I was on my way from the coffee shop to the operations office and noticed a Piper J3 Cub had a collapsed landing gear, which consisted of a heavy-duty duty rubber bungee cord connecting the tire assembly, which attached the landing gear assembly to the belly of the aircraft. The 6'2" young instructor climbed out of the front seat of this mini Cub and shook his head. His name was Dick Boyens and he resembled a young Charles Lindberg. Dick and I are still very good friends today. Dick followed my career by going to the FAA as an air traffic controller at LaGuardia Tower and then on to Northeast Airlines as a pilot. In the interim, Dick secured a job with Pepsi Cola as a first officer and was making some decent wages. Eventually, Dick quit and came to work for Northeast. However, it was quite a reduction in salary, as pilots only made $500 per month for the first year. Dick resigned from Northeast and went back to Pepsi. Sometime later, Dick was able to put his financial house in order and requested to be rehired by Northeast, which meant that Dick would have to start at the bottom of the seniority list once more. "Seniority" is the name of the game within pilot ranks. Captain Pete Loranger called and asked me if he should give Dick a second shot with Northeast. I told Pete that Dick was a sharp boy with great experience (not like some of us... I resemble that remark, and that he would be an asset to Northeast Airlines. Dick was hired. Unfortunately, Dick had to go out on a medical leave of absence early in his career.

My second instructor, Will Dodd, really inspired and helped me to stick with it. He was a former US Air Force pilot who flew P51s in Korea. He had the patience of a saint and a great personality. Will was responsible for me getting through my private pilot's license. Will instructed me through my first solo flight and taught me many things pertinent to the J3 Cub, which included flying the Cub backwards in a strong head wind above the stall speed of the aircraft, which was about 39 MPH. You would head directly into the wind and elevate the nose to just about the stall speed of the aircraft. With the headwind above the stall speed of the aircraft your path across the ground was backwards and you would be climbing. Flight is a function of airspeed and not groundspeed. Our paths crossed again, when we met as air traffic controllers in New York Center in 1963.

I developed a friendship with a "ramp rat" and fellow flight student from Deep River, CT named Richard Calarco. We worked together on the ramp, in crew scheduling and flight dispatch. We also took our instrument flight instruction together from Mrs. Jean Boice at Watson Aviation at Teterboro, NJ. Dick was my first passenger from Zahn's to Chester, CT, upon receiving my private pilot's license. Even to this day, we talk constantly; Dick lives just north of Portland, OR. I received my private pilot's license on September 07, 1958 and my commercial pilot's license on October 29, 1959. I had the honor of receiving my commercial flight check ride with Mr. Ed Lyons, a co-owner of Amityville Flying Service and one of the aviation pioneers on Long Island. He was a big stocky man who needed a shoehorn to get him in and out of a Piper J3 Cub. Ed had a bad back; however, he could fly the pants off that Piper Cub.

One thing that I learned during that check ride was how to get in and out of an *"over the top"* spin... a cross-controlled accelerated stall that becomes a spin.

It is an FAA requirement that a pilot must obtain a flight physical from an FAA approved doctor every three years for a third class physical (Private pilot) and every two years for a second class physical (commercial pilot) and every year for a first class physical (airline captain). The first class physical is the most stringent and includes a cardiogram after age thirty-five. In October of 1959, I needed to upgrade to a class two physical. Since I was employed at Idlewild/Kennedy Airport, I decided to go to the medical center on the airport for my second class physical. The medical center was under the supervision of Doctor Starr from Montauk Point. The physicals consist of a blood pressure check, depth perception, urine analysis, hearing and eye examinations… to name a few. At this center, a registered nurse performed the above tests. Everything was fine, up to the eye exam. This eye exam consisted of viewing the letter C, in different positions and it was my task to advise the registered nurse where the opening of the letter C was located. I discovered that I was having difficulty with this examination and did not pass. The doctor instructed me to obtain a pair of glasses and return for a re-test. I was totally devastated…. I would not be a candidate for an airline pilot's position because of glasses. The airline industry then would not hire someone with glasses as a pilot. I decided to seek the assistance of an ophthalmologist in Richmond Hill, Queens. I was examined by the ophthalmologist and he stated that there was nothing wrong with my eyes. I asked him to put that in writing, which he did. I immediately returned to Doctor Starr's office and presented the letter. Doctor Starr had me read the eye chart again… this time I passed. Originally, the nurse did not have the "C machine" calibrated properly. During my entire career I did not require reading glasses until I was fifty-six years old. Since my retirement, I have had problems with my eyes, specifically "Macular Degeneration," a problem with the Retina; I also have a hearing loss of forty five percent in both ears. Specialists have told me that these problems are associated with my aviation career. In the early days, nothing was done to prevent these occupational hazards from occurring.

I received my instrument rating on March 02, 1960 from Watson Aviation at Teterboro Airport, NJ. The remainder of my pilot ratings came during my career within the airline industry. Ironically, after completing my instrument flight test, on the drive back to Idlewild

Airport to start my night shift with Northeast Airlines, I turned on the radio and *"The High and the Mighty"* was playing on WPAT from Patterson, NJ. This just blew me away. Many years later, I was playing saxophone with the Stuart, FL concert band and was playing themes from the movies; one included the theme from ***"The High and the Mighty,"*** which flashed me back to Teterboro, NJ.

Payment for my flight training, which took me through my private and commercial pilot's licenses, came from the GI Bill of Rights. I supplemented this with my salary from Northeast Airlines. My Uncle John Ward loaned me the money to pay for my instrument rating. I paid the last $200 from the *envelopes* received at my wedding.

Another very influential person during my early years of aviation was New York Chief Pilot, Roland O. Loranger of Northeast Airlines, also known as Pete. He was from Manchester, NH. And his claim to fame was that he went to school with Grace Metalious who wrote Payton Place. Pete was a member of Northeast Airlines' contribution to the Army Air Corps, Air Transport Command and the European Division, whose escapades are recounted in movies, such as *" Island in The Sky"* This movie is a true story about a Northeast crew captained by Fred Lord and which starred John Wayne and Andy Devine, It was written by Ernest K. Gann who also gave us *"Fate is The Hunter"* and *"The High and The Mighty."* I worked for Pete when he was Chief Pilot in New York and I was a crew scheduler. It was our job to see that every flight had a full compliment of crewmembers, consisting of pilots and stewardesses (now known as flight attendants). Pete and I became very close; he gave me the nickname, "Mini Ginny." I loved him like a father.

I was only twenty-two years old and he would have me drive his orange and white 1956 Chevy Corvette convertible from the hangar to the gate to pick him up after a flight. This was the highlight of my life at that point in time. I thought to myself, *"Good golly, Miss Molly, pilots have it made."* Incidentally, I have never owned a sports car. Pete also helped in my attempt to become an airline pilot by furnishing me with the proper information and guidance so that I would make the right decisions at the appropriate time.

I mustn't forget to mention a flight engineer for Northeast Airlines in the 1960s by the name of Herb Thuemmler. Herb invited me to his home in Miami in 1961 and prepped me in the subjects needed to pass the CAA/FAA flight engineer written exam. At that time, this was an essential requirement when seeking employment as an airline pilot, since you had to start as a flight engineer. It was a five-part test, which included aircraft engines. At that point, they were reciprocating piston engines utilizing gasoline for fuel. Initially, I failed two parts; however, on the retake, I passed the ones that I missed the first time. This was the vital document permitting me to become a Northeast Airlines pilot on October 04, 1965, since I had very little flight time accumulated. Western Airlines eventually hired both Dick Calarco and Herb Theummler. We joined forces at Delta Air Lines in 1987 through the Delta/Western merger.

On April 20, 1960, I started acquiring flight time toward my flight instructor's rating with Harry McGinnis at Amityville Flight Service. One of the requirements for a flight instructor was to demonstrate spins; for this you had to wear a parachute. We were utilizing a PA18, Piper Super Cub for the training. We would climb to 5,000 feet and execute the spins over Deer Park Airport that was five miles northeast of Zahn's. One day, while executing a series of spins the nose cowling that was fastened with four Dzus quick disconnect fasteners became dislodged from the engine mount as we pitched down in the spin. The cowling, was also held on by a piano hinge, became loose but remained with the aircraft. The cowling flipped back and was resting on the windshield. We slowed down to a minimum controllable airspeed and spiraled down to a safe landing at Deer Park Airport. We did not have to use our parachutes. We had the cowling repaired and proceeded very cautiously back to Zahn's. This was an extremely anxious experience for me and taught me to become analytical and methodical.

I joined the Nassau Composite Squadron of the Civil Air Patrol and had the distinct honor of saluting my uncle, Captain Karl T. Hallberg, who was the US Air Force Liaison Officer to the CAP in Nassau County, Long Island, NY. It was my duty to fly a 150 horsepower Piper Super Cub from Zahn's Airport on Long Island. Our main mission was search and rescue and to provide familiarization flights to CAP officers and cadets. We were required to wear an Air Force flight suit. One of the mechanics for Northeast Airlines, Stanley Weidenbaum, who worked with me at Idlewild/JFK, owned an airplane at Zahn's Airport. When he saw me in the flight suit, I acquired the name, "Sky King."

A funny story just came to mind about Stanley; he was trying to get hired by Northeast Airlines as a pilot as I was. Unfortunately, Stanley had a medical problem, which precluded "pilot" as a profession. Stanley stuttered and for that reason was passed over. Stanley was quite angry and rightfully so. When Stanley was asked why he was not hired, he would say, "The r-r-r-reason that I didn't g-g-get h-h-hired was because I was J-J-J- Jewish."

One afternoon, I was assigned to give a CAP senior member a familiarization flight out of Zahn's. The person who showed up was a female. Normally it would not be a problem; but she did not have the required flight suit. To complicate matters, she was wearing a skin-tight skirt, which in a tandem duel control stick cockpit aircraft, presented a problem. I was hesitant to take her up; she assured me that it would not create a problem. I ran her through a preflight check and made sure that she was as comfortable as possible with her tight skirt and the control stick. The aircraft checked out ok, but I discovered a little opposition on the stick when I checked the flight controls for freedom of movement. I decided this would not be a problem. We took off to the south at Zahn's and proceeded over Fire Island and followed the barrier island to the south. She was feeling a little uncomfortable, so I decided to return to Zahn's for a landing. On our descent, I realized that there was quite a bit of opposition to my elevator inputs. I turned around to see what the problem was and discovered that this female CAP officer was sitting sidesaddle! I was not about to do anything that might jeopardize the flight, so I eased it down to the runway without any abnormal or excessive elevator inputs and lived happily ever after. Moral of the story, don't wear tight skirts in a tandem duel controlled aircraft.

The CAP, in conjunction with the 514 Troop Carrier Wing, arranged that we would take some cadets for a familiarization ride in a C119 Flying Box Car out of Mitchell Field. Two of Northeast Airlines pilots, Captain John Stumpf and First Officer Frank Santo, flew with the 514th. We loaded about twenty kids in the Box Car and proceeded to the run up area for takeoff. The magneto check was not satisfactory, so we returned to the gate to change planes. We finally took off and were flying visually around Long Island. The weather was a little turbulent causing the aircraft to yaw and made the kids sick. We returned to base and called it a day.

On December 16, 1960, I received permission to ride the jump seat (a seat in the cockpit) from LGA to BOS for a pilot interview on a Northeast Airlines Vickers Viscount. This was a four engine turbo prop aircraft, which was used by Northeast as a shuttle between Washington, LaGuardia and Boston. I was on the 09:30 shuttle between LGA and BOS, the captain was Ed Butler and the stewardess was Joan Ortyl, who would eventually marry Ed Butler. It was snowing as we took off on runway 31. When we landed in Boston, we learned that there was a midair collision over Brooklyn, at Sterling Place to be exact; it involved a TWA Lockheed Constellation and a United DC8. I learned subsequent to the crash that the United was holding at an intersection over Rumson, NJ and jumped the holding pattern due to a cockpit radio navigational failure. As a result of that midair collision the FAA instituted a 250-knot airspeed restriction below 10,000, which is still in effect today. Sadly, I did not get the pilot position at that time. I continued on with the flight instructor's rating until July 20, 1961. I then turned all my attention to preparation for the FAA flight engineer written exam with Herb Theummler in Miami.

Ultimately, I was offered two flying jobs, one with Western Airlines, where I had gone for an interview in 1961 and one with Eastern in 1962. I refused both offers because my new bride did not want me to fly. I was married on September 16, 1962 at St. Benedict Joseph Labre Catholic Church in Richmond Hill, Queens.

I was reassigned back to passenger service at Idlewild on November 30, 1962, and worked the four to midnight shift. The weather was quite bad, with low visibility due to fog. Fog is quite prevalent at Idlewild/JFK due to the airport's close proximity to the Atlantic Ocean. I was working a Convair 880 that was in the final stages for a flight to Miami. As I was in the process of closing out the flight, we received word that there would be a delay because Idlewild's weather was below *"minimums"* due to fog. I was on the ramp near the front cabin door when I heard a piston aircraft engines rev up. I did not hear a crash, but we were advised that the airport was closed due to a crash on runway 4R. We were told that it was an Eastern DC7 that crashed on an attempted go around.

The next scenario is something quite hilarious and depicts a scene of a "Keystone Kops" silent movie. One of the duties of ground personnel is to service the lavatories onboard each aircraft. This consists of emptying the lavatory holding tanks and sanitizing the entire lavatory unit. There is a specially designed tank truck with a flexible six-inch hose that connects to the underside of the aircraft below each lavatory that relieves the holding tank of its contents. The name given this truck is the *"honey bucket truck."* This was the responsibility of one person, who in this scenario was Hector., who was fired for some unknown reason. Subsequent to his firing, the *"honey bucket truck"* disappeared from the airport and about two weeks later was discovered on Cropsy Avenue in Brooklyn. The truck was returned and pressed into service once more. Another night, I was working on the ramp under the direction of supervisor Louie DellaBovie. It was at the end of my four to twelve shift and I was instructed to have the equipment washed and readied for the morning shift. As I approached the *"honey bucket truck,"* I saw Hector jump into the driver's seat, take off on a taxi way and head for the airport exit. I brought this to Mr. DellaBovie's attention. He immediately jumped into the first available vehicle, instructed me to get in the back and proceeded to chase Hector and the *"honey bucket truck"* around the airport. It appears that *"Hector was on the loose."* The truck Mr. DellaBovie chose was a ramp truck, which has a telescoping ramp that adjusts to accommodate various aircraft. Picture this scene: I am on the back of the ramp truck holding on for dear life, while Louie and the ramp truck are twisting and weaving, nearly turning over a number of times, chasing the *"honey bucket truck"* all over the confines of Idlewild/JFK Airport. Hector escaped once more, since those vehicles were only permitted and licensed to operate on Port of NY Authority property. The *"honey bucket truck"* was again discovered on Cropsy Avenue and eventually Hector was arrested on the charge of *"unlawful use of a honey bucket truck on New York City streets."* Thanks to good old Hector, I had the ride of my life. Case closed.

One cold February morning, I was invited to go up in a seaplane piloted by a co-worker and friend, Irwin Cooperman. We both worked for Northeast Airlines in Ground Operations; we both went to the FAA as air traffic controllers, Coop at Idlewild/Kennedy Tower and me at New York Center. Eventually, Northeast Air Lines hired us both as pilots. We are still friends today. The aircraft was just out of overhaul and had to be test flown. The seaplane base was located at Mill Basin in Brooklyn NY, which ran parallel to Flatbush Avenue. The aircraft being tested was a Piper Cub on floats. Incidentally, the floats were made by the EDO Corporation located in College Point, Queens, which is adjacent to

LaGuardia Airport. This aircraft did not have an electric starter; like other small aircraft it had to be "*propped*," or started by hand. We took off and headed in an easterly direction towards Canarsie in Brooklyn, which is just to the west of JFK. We were down below two hundred feet when the engine quit. Coop set it down on Jamaica Bay, opened the cowl and checked things out; he stood on the pontoon and propped from behind. We got it started and flew it back to the Brooklyn seaplane base... I haven't been in a seaplane since.

Chapter Nine:

Federal Aviation Agency Air Route Traffic Control Center, New York February 23, 1963 to October 03, 1965

I remained with Northeast Airlines until February 1963; I then went to work as an air traffic controller in New York Center for the FAA. The position was contingent upon passing and completing the requirements of the Federal Aviation Academy. It was a difficult six-month concentrated course that twenty-five percent of the participants *"washed out."* From the instructor I learned to "admit nothing, deny everything, and demand proof."

Once my training was complete in August of 1963, I decided to have a home built on Long Island since New York Center would be moving to its new headquarters at Long Island Macarthur Airport in Lake Ronkonkoma, NY. My wife gave birth to our first child, a son on October 03, 1963. He passed away eighteen hours into his life, and we were both completely shattered. Subsequently, my wife gave birth to two wonderful daughters, Linda Anne and Leslie Anne, of whom we are quite proud.

My work was quite interesting and the crew with whom I worked included some great guys. Lee Biggio was one of the radar controllers on my crew; he was a real sharp controller, a great guy and the father of the Houston Astros' second baseman, Craig Biggio, who will be inducted into the Baseball Hall of Fame.

On the day that President John F. Kennedy was assassinated, I was working the flight data position at New York Center. The flight data position was a liaison position, in which you would receive and process flight plans from pilots and answer telephone communications when the need arose. I received the telephone call from FAA Headquarters in Washington that the president had been shot and had eventually died. I learned also that the country was in *"Defense Condition Five,"* which is quite serious.

In 1964, I was awarded the "FAA sustained superior performance" rating, which meant that my performance was over and above the call of duty. However, during this period of time in my life, I still had the greatest desire to fly with an airline.

On a dark and horrible snowy and windy winter night following a cold frontal passage, I was working with my crew on sector 14, which were LaGuardia and Newark departures. It was quite busy and there was no time for a break, whatsoever. About eight o'clock that night, we received flight data, consisting of a flight strip that provided us with the call sign of the aircraft, type of aircraft, flight plan which consisted of departure point, destination, assigned altitude and ETA, (estimated time of arrival) at fixes within our area of jurisdiction, on a Cessna 182. The aircraft's destination was Norwood, MA, about 17 nautical miles southwest of Boston. The aircraft contacted us via VHF (very high frequency) radio and stating that he was concerned about fuel consumption. We advised the flight that there was a line of heavy thunderstorms with moderate to severe turbulence associated with the cold front and, at that point in time; it would be impossible for him to penetrate the frontal boundary safely. We asked what was his intention? He stated, "Stand By." As he progressed through our area, the weather worsened and the pilot had his hands full and started to panic. We suggested that he make a 180 degree turn (reverse course) and land at the nearest suitable airport. At this, the pilot became totally incoherent. The controller on our crew stated, "For the safety of your aircraft and its occupants, turn left to a heading of 320 degrees and proceed on radar vectors to the Westchester Airport." The pilot acknowledged the instructions and was transferred to another controller. About two hours later the watch supervisor at the FAA air traffic control facility at Islip received a telephone call thanking us for helping him make the right decision. Everything that goes well ends well.

In June of 1965, both my wife and I were invited to a neighbor Sal's home for a barbecue. During the festivities, my neighbor asked my wife how she liked flying, since she was a stewardess with Northeast Airlines. She said that she loved it. With that, I decided I would seriously pursue my lifelong dream of becoming an airline pilot. The one saying that was a driving force throughout my life and career was, ***"The sorriest words of tongue and pen, is that it might have been."*** And still is. I decided to journey to Kennedy Airport and speak with the FAA about studying and obtaining my airline flight dispatcher's rating, which would help me obtain a position with a major airline. The FAA approved my request. While at the airport, I visited the Northeast Airlines flight operations office. I walked in and my former boss, Captain Pete Loranger, just happened to be there. Incidentally, I believe in happenstance. Normally, chief pilots fly and give other pilots "line checks," which are required by the FAA once a year. They are rarely in the office. The "line checks" consist of observing a pilot's performance in the air and assuring that he or she is conforming to company and FAA procedures.

Pete greeted me with, "Where the Hell have you been, Mini Ginny?" This was an old term of endearment. I told him that I was an air traffic controller at NY Center. He asked, "Do you want to fly?" I was totally dumbfounded. Pete told me that Northeast Airlines just purchased twenty-three jets from Boeing and Douglas; consisting of B727-100 & 200 series from Boeing and DC9s from Douglas and required approximately 500 new hire pilots, post haste. Pete told me to get my ass outside and call Boston now. This was Friday afternoon. I called to speak to the chief pilot. Captain Lloyd Fiske answered the telephone and was very gracious; he remembered me. I said that I would like to come to Boston for an interview. Captain Fiske was quite receptive and we agreed that I would come up Monday. I asked if I could possibly get a pass and he answered in the affirmative. Monday, I called in sick with the FAA and flew to Boston to meet with Captain Clancy. The interview went quite well, even though I was a nervous wreck. Upon returning home, there were so many things I had to do; for example; log books and a first class FAA medical exam, which included a cardiogram, etc. Life settled back to normal. Two months went by and I didn't hear from Northeast. I assumed that I had been passed over. On September 10, 1965, I received a request to report to Massachusetts General Hospital for a physical. I reported to Dr. Parkhurst and survived a four hour physical. The only thing left was a cardiogram. I was unable to receive the cardiogram because it was Rosh Hashanah, a Jewish high holy day and there was no one available to give me the cardiogram. I stated that I was unable to return and that it had to be done "today." Luckily, they found someone qualified to administer the EKG. I returned and things were back to normal once more. I didn't hear anything pertaining to the results of the physical, so gloom and doom reared its ugly head.

On September 22, 1965 at 16:15, I was outside setting posts for a fence when my wife called me and announced that I had a telephone call. I was encrusted with creosote and answered the phone gingerly. It was Western Union stating that it had a telegram from Northeast Airlines and would I care if it were read to me initially over the phone? It was the news I had been waiting for; I was to start school in Boston on October 04, 1965…coincidentally, the same day that Pope Paul came to America. I had only twelve days to report to Boston, less than the required two weeks' notice of employment termination required by the FAA. But, there was nothing that was going to stop me now, "Come Hell or High Water."

Chapter Ten:

Northeast Airlines Flight Training, October 04, 1965 to October 27, 1965

Let the festivities begin.

I rented a room in a private home in Winthrop, which was a suburb just off the airport property in Boston. I reported to the Northeast hangar on October 04, 1965 at 08:00, a day that will be part of me forever. There were twenty new hires in the first class that Northeast Airlines hired since 1961; we were all at the right place at the right time. Seniority was determined by age. I was twenty-nine and number seven in my class. Captain Clancy addressed the class and asked if anyone had the flight engineer rating. There were no *"ayes."* Captain Clancy's next question asked, was how many pilots had passed the flight engineer's written exam? There were six of us. Captain Clancy stated that we would be DC3 first officers, of whom I was one scared puppy. I lucked out again, thanks to Herb Theummler. Evidently, Northeast needed immediate replacements to train on the jet fleet that was coming on board, and we were it.

We were assigned instructors; there were Captains Moran, Worth, and Perry. Each instructor was assigned two students. I was paired with Don Bartlett, and Captain Angus Perry was our instructor. Captain Perry was a super guy who became my friend and confidant for life; I miss him dearly. He was on my first flight with Northeast on October 28, 1965 and was there to greet me on my last flight on May 19 1996. The six of us, consisted of F/Os Moore and Gutierrez with Captain Moran, F/Os

Schmoyer and Pitts with Captain Worth and F/Os Bartlett and Gravino with Captain Perry. If it weren't for Captain Angus Perry, I would have never made it, due to my lack of experience.

We attended two weeks of ground school on the DC3, which had basic aircraft systems. During my first week in DC3 ground school, we encountered many Northeast pilots who were curious to see what *"the new kids on the block looked like."* One of these men was the illustrious Captain Hostile who recognized me immediately and stated, "I had better not ever get you in the right seat of my airplane." That comment put *"the fear of God"* in me. I had come all this way to be shot down by this vindictive imbecile. During my first year, a probationary period, I was deathly afraid that I would have to fly with this egotistical tyrant. Luckily, this did not occur; but stay tuned for the next episode of ***"The Adventures of Captain Hostile."*** After systems, we were turned over to Mrs. Liz Shedden and Mrs. Pat (Mother) Malone for operations specifications. This pertains to Federal Air Regulations, specifically Part 121, which deals with scheduled airline operations. We also received dehmal simulator training, basically, a non-maneuverable cockpit procedural trainer. It was a prehistoric monster compared to what we would be training in during the late 1990s. We received four hours of dehmal training and then were released to fly the DC3 Dakota or the Gooney Bird, also known by Captain Perry as "the swept wing multi-engine transport."

During my flight training, I developed a friendship with Ed Moore, who was also in the DC3 program. Ed was a real sharp pilot who lived at Montauk Point, NY. He managed the Sky Portal airport and Montauk Caribbean Airways and flew for Perry Duryea, a New York State politician and lobsterman. He flew me back to Long Island on weekends, so that I could spend time with my wife and newborn baby daughter.

Here's a little insight into my previous flying background. The biggest airplane I had ever flown prior to the DC3 was a Cessna 172, which was quite a while prior to October 18, 1965. Needless to say, I was quite scared and stale. Angus was a superb instructor and a great guy, totally aware of my lack of experience. Thankfully, he was impressed with my determination and dedication to my newfound career. I would go home and fly the maneuvers on my upside down kitchen chair. I had never flown an ILS (instrument landing system) with a glide slope, but with some common sense and some planning, it all fell into place. My partner, Don Bartlett, was having major difficulties and caused us to have to go back and fly the dehmal once more, which took its toll on me. Angus bestowed the nickname, Vic Tanney (the famous body building trainer) upon me, which would stay with me until Angus's passing on December 19, 2003. I received the name because when Angus reduced the power on one engine, the rudder pedal of the leg on the side of the functioning engine would shake from nerves and from not locking my foot into the floor of the cockpit to counteract the torque generated by the functioning engine and propeller. I lost a total of fifteen pounds during the eighteen days of flight training. We completed two more sessions in the dehmal and proceeded to fly the airplane once more. Evidentially, Don Bartlett could not get his act together; he would go home on his days off and party on his yacht. I, on the other hand, would hop on my kitchen chair and fly my fanny off. Thus, he was terminated, which was too bad, but great for me, *"**You snooze, you lose.**"* I finished up and flew my first line trip on October 28, 1965 with Angus Perry as Captain and Roseanne Vollinger as stewardess, from Boston to Hyannis and Nantucket and return. It was the greatest day of my life and my childhood dream was finally fulfilled. God Bless Angus Perry. The festivities were unfortunately, short lived.

Chapter Eleven:

Flying by the Seat of Your Pants, Northeast Airlines, October 28, 1965 to July 31, 1972

Upon completing my line check as a DC3 first officer, there was a message for me to call crew scheduling. I was assigned a trip leaving within one hour for a Burlington, VT overnight via Lebanon, NH. I was totally unprepared; it was winter and I had no overcoat or overnight suitcase. However, I could not refuse. I was assigned and I was the most junior qualified DC3 first officer on Northeast Airlines property. The trip consisted of Boston, Lebanon, NH and Burlington, VT and returns the next day. The captain did all the flying; I was there to assist him. I was " *the new kid on the block.*" The trip to Lebanon was uneventful. There were snow showers in the vicinity of Lebanon and to the northwest leading to Burlington. We broke out into the clear thirty miles southeast of Burlington, which is on the eastern shore of Lake Champlain. We were working air traffic control at Plattsburg approach control, an Air Force base in New York, across from Lake Champlain. We were on radar vectors landing runway 15 in Burlington. We were heading northwest bound with the runway off our right and were asked if we had the runway in sight. I learned early on not to say anything on the radio without the captain's approval; therefore, I asked the captain if he had the runway in sight and he said, " Yes." I then conveyed that to ATC. As a former air traffic controller, I expected the captain to make two ninety-degree right turns and land on runway 15 in Burlington; however, my fearless leader proceeded straight ahead.

I sensed that something was wrong; but I was too timid to say anything especially on my first flight. I figured ATC would pick it up on radar, which they did. It was apparent that the captain saw the runway at Plattsburg Air Force Base across the lake and was proceeding to that runway. Upon notification by ATC, the captain corrected his flight path and we landed without incident. That was another classic example of the value of local knowledge and situation awareness.

The winter months on the DC3 were a total education. The de-icing on the Gooney Bird (DC3) consisted of an inflatable bladder on the leading edge of the wing, which was activated with a manual on/off switch. The propeller anti-ice system consisted of alcohol. When the prop ice would eventually dislodge from the prop, it would impact the fuselage with a loud noise that sounded like a pistol shot. The first time I heard it, it startled me and I shouted "what the ---- was that?" The DC3 has reinforced aluminum sections on the fuselage to prevent damage from the propeller ice. The anti-icing consisted of two garden faucet type valves, which allowed alcohol to be sent to the slinger ring on each prop and the other to the forward windshield. It was really only effective in light icing. When you activated the windshield anti-ice system, you would get the alcohol fumes in the cockpit and experience the euphoria of " *The High and the Mighty.*"

On November 01, 1965, my first flight sequence out of the New York domicile started with NE 308 from LGA, BOS via EWB and HYA. In English, that is LaGuardia to Boston via New Bedford and Hyannis. I remember it vividly. The captain was Frank Davis and the stewardess was Loraine Tracy. I knew both from my crew scheduling days. Frank Davis lived in Watertown, MA. Frank had flown me over his home, which was north of Boston on a later trip. This was customary in those days; we were permitted to fly VFR (visual flight rules) when the weather was good; we took the scenic route. Loraine Tracy was from Massachusetts, but lived in the Miami area. My DC3 flying consisted exclusively of flights through Connecticut, Rhode Island, Massachusetts, New Hampshire, Vermont, and Maine. This was great experience for me, especially in winter. I flew with some great instructor pilots who taught me to fly by the seat of my pants and to use common sense and wisdom, coupled with local knowledge and situation awareness that would become invaluable in all my years as a captain.

Local knowledge was utilized when the weather was marginal, VFR vs. IFR, (visual flight rules vs. instrument flight rules.) It was used in conjunction with known familiar objects on the ground. For instance, when you saw farmer Jones' water tower; you make a turn to the published runway heading of the airport of intended landing, which would put you on an extended final approach to that runway/airport. This and situation awareness are the two most important assets in a pilot's bag of tricks.

During my first year probation on the DC3, I met many new friends and some old acquaintances from my ground days with Northeast. I will give honorable mention to a few; however, if I don't get to you all, please know you are still embedded in my heart. On the DC3 out of New York, there was Captain John Stumpf and his wife, Madge and their late son John, who were my neighbors on Long Island. My young daughters called him Uncle John. There was Captain Dick Barnes; I had my first mechanical problem with him in Hartford, CT on the DC3 due to a faulty magneto. Then there was Captain Norm Houle. While flying with him on the DC3, we hit a NY seagull after departing runway 31 at LGA. Coincidentally, Eastern instituted a new advertisement in the newspaper, depicting a seagull in the landing configuration. We sent the article to each other. Through the years, whenever we saw each other, we would say, "Hit any seagulls lately?" Here is one of my corny jokes, "If a seagull flies over the sea, what flies over Jamaica Bay? And, the answer is… "a Jamaica Bay Gull."

Then there was the late Captain Guy Caron, who I called the "French Supreme Allied Commander." He almost got me fired by flying over Marshfield MA, too low. There was also the infamous Captain Tom Twomey; I will not *"go there,"* except to say that he was an MIT graduate and a genius. There was Captain Bill Kenny who flew with my wife and was a super guy. There was Captain George Chaudoin and his wife Ann, a neighbor from Stony Brook, NY, two super people who now live in New Hampshire. George does an outstanding job, keeping us informed on current affairs, even now that we are retired. Thanks George. There was also Captain Walt Schneider and his wife Helen, who was a stewardess, another real great couple. Then there was "Microphone Mike," last name omitted. He was honored with that name because he enjoyed keeping everyone informed of their location and some little known facts about the ground below. For instance, the Verazzano Narrows Bridge; he gave it a totally different name. He would make ten PA's (public addresses) between Boston and New York at 02:00. One night on a B727 at 22:00 approaching JFK over Long Beach, Long Island, Microphone Mike was cleared to change radio frequencies to JFK Control Tower. Mike changed frequency and on his initial contact to JFK Tower stated, "Kennedy Tower, this is Northeast 626, over 'Timothy Tubbs' with a candle in the window," which in English is NE 626 is over his favorite watering hole in Long Beach, Long Island, on the approach to runway 31R with a landing light on. It was customary that the pilot not flying would make the PA announcement, not in Mike's world… he made all the PA's.

There were some other great gentlemen with whom I flew out of New York on the B727; I have a soft place in my heart for them. Unfortunately, they are almost all gone now. There was Captain James Mapes Dodge of Pound Ridge, NY, originally of the "Main Line" of Philadelphia; Captain Walt Byers of Huntington, NY, a WWII fighter pilot, a great guy and a great pilot. His claim to fame was he liked to sing one particular song from the 40s and alter the words a tad, to "Tangerine, you are my sex machine." There was Captain John Plack and his lovely wife Betty. John's greeting when he saw you was always, "Plack's back." One of the first and finest "gentlemen captains" who upgraded to jets was Captain Fred Lane. Fred is now in his 90's and still going strong. Northeast Airlines had leased a Boeing 707 from Trans World Airlines in the late 70's and Fred flew the New York to Miami route out of Idlewild Airport. One other great guy was a five-foot-two Italian named Lou Singrossi. I remember him and his wife Marie...they were from Huntington, Long Island. Lou started out with NE on the ground, like many of us. Lou was an aircraft mechanic turned pilot. He looked, spoke, acted and smoked cigars exactly like Edward G. Robinson. In 1970 I was awarded a Boeing 727 first officer bid with Captain Singrossi, myself as first officer and George Ferdinand as flight engineer. The three of us were native New Yorkers. The captain lived in an up-scale neighborhood in Dix Hills, I lived in Centereach and the flight engineer lived in Patchogue. We flew a trip that left at 17:00 for Fort Lauderdale and returned the same evening at 23:45 It was quite an economical trip in that there was no overnight, which relieved the airline of the added expenses of providing hotels and meal allowance for its flight crew. The airlines of today should take some lessons from the airlines of yesteryear on how to reduce operating costs. Lou was quite a guy. His brother-in-law named Frank, lived in Ft. Lauderdale. He would meet us between flights for dinner. Lou always picked up the tab. We visited an Italian restaurant on Las Olas Boulevard in Ft. Lauderdale where the owner/chef greeted us at the door. Lou and the owner/chef conversed in Italian. The chef concocted his version of Fettuccini Alfredo using ricotta cheese especially for us. The dish was out of this world. Lou sent the chef a glass of the restaurant's best wine, which is an Italian custom. The chef returned the favor; however, we had to decline as we were flying back to New York. A great time was had by all. We would also go to Dania Jai Alai, which is a form of Latin handball with an elongated glove made of straw. We did this flight sequence four times a week. On one of these round trips, we decided to bring some food from home, as we were all lovers of Italian food. The next night, we brought in the ingredients for a Caesar Salad and Clams on the half shell with cocktail sauce, etc. The dining area was quite cramped and only one person could eat at a time. The aroma of garlic and the other ingredients wafted throughout the cramped quarters of our Boeing 727 cockpit. It sure beats the airline cuisine of yesterday and today's "Nuts to you, sir". I followed this procedure for the rest of my thirty plus year career. There was also a great friend, Captain Karl Wallace from Islandia, Long Island who deserves some ink. I loved the New York base and all the colorful people in it. I can't forget Captain Broadway Joe Sheehan, a former actor, turned pilot and his wife Nadia from New Canaan, CT. One other great pilot and friend is Captain Barney Sonin of Englewood Cliffs, NJ who resides in Ft. Lauderdale and is now an air carrier inspector with the FAA. Barney acquired the moniker " Mr. Peepers," but I called him "The Bookworm," from the Batman character with the tensor light mounted to his forehead. Barney carried a pad with every calculation pertaining to rates of decent, fuel flows, true air speeds, and the phone numbers of every available stewardess in the NY base " *just kidding.*" We had a captain in New York named Frank Lage, who incidentally went to my high school; we called him, "*Frank Lage, the flying rage.*" Sadly, Frank met with an untimely death… his second wife stabbed him and "*she walked.*" One of my classmates and his wife went through a horrendous ordeal with a member of their family, which garnered the attention of the nation and is still ongoing. I will not go there. My heart goes out to both of them.

"Adventures of a Yellowbird"

During the late 60s and early 70s there was severe competition on the New York to Miami, Ft. Lauderdale, Palm Beach and the Bahamas routes. There was Northeast Airlines' "Yellowbird" aggressive advertising campaign. It consisted of yellow and white aircraft, flight attendants in iridescent lime green hot pants outfits and the song "Yellowbird" played by a calypso band equipped with steel drums. In Nassau in the Bahamas the Blind Blake Trio treated us to their native music and dancers. The words were altered to reflect the new Northeast Airlines' advertising campaign, which became quite a concern of the competition. When we got in range of either Nassau or Freeport, we contacted the company radio with a liquor order for Butler and Sands, a local distributor who gave us a sizable discount, i.e. an Imperial Quart (forty ounces) of Dewar's Scotch cost only $5.75 U.S. ...at that time, a great savings.

Eastern Airlines and National Airlines flew on the same routes. Both Eastern and National had their corporate headquarters in Miami, while Northeast was headquartered in Boston. Northeast was considered an interloper. Both National and Eastern received alleged preferential treatment pertaining to ATC (air traffic control). There were rumors that came Christmas time; Miami Center (ATC) would receive gifts from anonymous donors. It seems that at 21:00 every night, there seemed to be a mass exodus to New York from Southern Florida. A group of flights namely Northeast, Eastern and National pushed back from the gate in Miami and Ft. Lauderdale utilizing Control 1150 (the airway off shore between Bimini and Cape Fear, NC (Wilmington, NC) and take off in "formation," so to speak. It was quite a hassle to obtain the optimum route and altitude, taking into consideration prevailing winds, turbulence, etc, factors of the jet stream and cloud cover. In the wintertime, due to the jet stream dipping south out of Canada, you could expect as much as a one hundred and twenty knot head wind going southwest and the same amount of tailwind going northeast. The jet core (center of the jet stream) was usually about thirty three thousand feet. Incidentally, one knot equals fifteen percent above a statute mile or one hundred knots equals one hundred and fifteen miles per hour. The name of the game was to get the most efficient altitude, taking into consideration the amount of tailwind or headwind. The main factors here were turbulence for passenger comfort and the structural effect on the aircraft. This is where blind trust (relying on someone else) comes into play. For instance, the aircraft dispatcher, who is responsible for flight planning the individual flight, including the most economical route and supplying a fuel load that takes into consideration the fuel required to destination, plus fuel required if there is inclement weather for holding, plus fuel to an alternate airport, plus an additional forty five minutes as a safety factor. Meteorology also comes into play here, so that in the final analysis, the captain and the dispatcher put their heads together and agree on a plan of action and a route of flight. Both the captain and the dispatcher sign their names to the pertinent documents and take full responsibility for the safety of those associated with the particular flight. In the final analysis, the captain is ultimately responsible. Enough of **Flight Planning 101.** Now back to the scenario. The main goal here was to push back on time and get to the head of the pack, so that you received the most expeditious route and preferential altitude. This is where my previous experience as an air traffic controller became an absolute benefit. As a first officer, I'd get on the aircraft as soon as everyone was off the aircraft from the inbound flight and call for an Air Traffic Control clearance to our destination plus the desired requested optimum altitude. Thanks to my skill and planning, I'd get the altitude and route from Miami to New York's International Airport. One particular night, we pushed back from the gate on time and were number one for takeoff. On departure, it is a requirement to maintain two hundred fifty knots below ten thousand feet and then go to an optimum airspeed, which was three hundred forty knots until attaining an optimum mach number (M) of M.78 for climb and then M.82 for cruise (a percentage of the speed of sound) which you would use for cruise. We climbed to flight level three five zero (FL 35,000 feet); up to 17,999 feet you use a local altimeter setting. At 18,000 and above you set your altimeter to a standard barometric pressure of 29.92 inches of mercury at sea level and 59 degrees of Fahrenheit, temperature wise. At that time, there was a required separation of two thousand feet. Therefore, Yellowbird was at FL350, Eastern was at FL 330 and National was at FL310. We were experiencing a relatively smooth ride while Eastern and National were getting quite a bit more turbulence and had to slow to their turbulence penetration speed, or M.78. We were receiving a one hundred twenty knot tailwind, due to the jet stream, which equated to four hundred and eighty knots true airspeed and one hundred twenty knot tailwind. We were hauling at a grand total of six hundred knot ground speed, which equates to ten nautical miles a minute or six hundred and ninety statute miles per hour. In reality you are, "Hauling Ass." After quite a bit of frustration on the part of the Eastern flight, the pilot stated, "Why do I have to stay below this Damn Yellowbird? Evidentially, there was another Yellowbird on the same air traffic control discrete radio frequency and he stated, "Don't ever get under a Yellowbird. FYI, it normally takes two hours and twenty minutes airtime from Miami to New York. With this divine tailwind, we made it in one hour and fifty-two minutes airtime. The nautical mileage from Miami to NY/JFK is 1090, therefore, you divide one hour and fifty-two minutes or 1.9 - (which is one and nine tenths of an hour) and that equates to 573.68 knots or 659.74 miles per hour, which is close to the speed of sound and close to a speed record. There is a French Aviation Organization known as Federeration Aeronautique Internationale (FAI), which sets and oversees the standards for the establishment of aviation speed records. They are broken down into numerous categories and are quite interesting.

If you wish to learn more about this endeavor, go to the following Website, http://records.fai.org/generalaviation/ which is the FAI web site or you can go to http://en.wikipedia.org/wiki/Flight_airspeed_record. Both sites are quite interesting and you will enjoy the trip and the statistics.

To summarize my flying career, I spent one year on the DC3 as first officer, one year as first officer on the FH227, which was the replacement to the DC3, a more reliable aircraft. For me, the DC3 was quite a learning experience, in that it introduced me to actual instrument flying conditions and to low visibility approaches and landings, runway conditions and mountainous terrain. By runway conditions, I mean wet, snowy, and icy runways. It tested my mettle in landings and takeoffs in high wind conditions and crosswind conditions. The guys with whom I flew were great pilots and instructors. This type of flying separated the men from the boys. The Fairchild was a completely pneumatic aircraft with electric flaps that created problems. Normally, aircraft have hydraulic gears, flaps, and brakes that are more reliable. The Fairchild was underpowered and was limited regarding payload. One incident involving this aircraft that I would like to bring to light is, ***The Adventures of Captain Hostile.*** This was my first and thankfully last encounter with this illustrious individual.

I was flying Fairchild FH227 as first officer out of New York, which was the junior base. Because of an illness, crew scheduling sent Captain Hostile to New York to fly the two-day sequence. He saw me and immediately had a flashback to the incident in which I had to write him up. The two-day sequence was subsequently filled with critiques of my flying ability. Pilots have the philosophy that they and only they are the world's greatest and everyone else is substandard. My philosophy as a captain was "*We all fly differently and have different habits; however, if you are safe and fly by the book, there is nothing to critique,*" Captain Hostile, on the other hand, was out to get me, no question about it. I was not the greatest pilot and far from the worst. On retirement, I flew a total of thirty and one half years, without an incident; that is more than I can say about many other professionals. Captain Hostile critiqued everything under the sun and it finally got on my nerves. I did not say a thing; however, on the last day with only two legs to fly, we were going from Keene, NH to Lebanon, NH, a distance of seventy-five miles. The illustrious captain was flying. The weather was perfect VFR (Visual Flight Rules), no ATC (Air Traffic Control) clearance needed. We were at 3,500 feet and approximately thirty miles southwest of Lebanon when Captain Hostile, who flew this area for many, many years, made the mistake of thinking the Claremont airport was the Lebanon, NH Airport. Claremont is 19.6 DME (Distance Measuring Equipment) southwest of the Lebanon VOR (Visual Omni Range). As he made his approach to the airport, I had my VOR (visual omni range) tuned to Lebanon and I didn't say anything. Captain Hostile turned final to runway 29 (290 Degrees Magnetic), Lebanon's runway is runway 25 (250 Degrees Magnetic)). We approached the airport at 1,500 AGL (Above Ground Level) I said, "Do you really want to land there, Captain?" He answered, "Yes, why." I said, "This is Claremont." With that, Captain Hostile wiped the egg off his face, executed a missed approach, and departed for Lebanon, never to be heard from again. For the rest of his career, every time I saw him, I would say, "That doesn't look like Lebanon to me, Captain." Payback is a bitch. End of a saga and the end of "***The Adventures of Captain Hostile.***"

Upon completion of a year on probation, I joined the Airline Pilots' Association, which represented the pilots for the major airlines in the industry. I became the first officer representative of ALPA (Airline Pilots Association) for the New York Council for Northeast Airlines. We all attended a three-day union seminar in Bermuda... a waste of money, wouldn't you say? In the latter part of 1967, I was asked to attend a meeting as an ALPA representative with New York Air Traffic Controllers, in as much as I was a former air traffic controller from New York Center. It was pertaining to the air traffic controllers forming a union known as PATCO (Professional Air Traffic Controllers Organization.) It was held at the LaGuardia Airport Cafeteria. In attendance was Mike Rock who I knew from New York Center, and was now an air traffic controller at LaGuardia Tower. Also in attendance was Dick Smith from LaGuardia tower. PATCO was seeking affiliation with ALPA. I took notes pertaining to their requests and forwarded them to ALPA National in Washington, D.C. J. J. Donnell of Eastern Airlines was president at that time. PATCO was formed in May 1968 in an affiliation with the Maritime Engineers Union (MEBA). F. Lee Bailey was selected as Executive Director and John Leyden, who I knew from New York Center, was his assistant. In 1970 PATCO staged a sick out and I attended some of their meetings and rallies. They were quite militant. During the sick out, I was asked by ALPA to visit New York Center and evaluate the quality of the air traffic control service coupled with the staffing involved. I attended with Lee Alexander from the Allied Pilots' Association representing American Airlines. Once again, I wrote up a report on my findings and submitted it to J. J.O'Donnell. John Leyden, who was a fine gentleman, replaced F. Lee Bailey as director of PATCO; Robert Polli replaced John in 1980. In 1981, the Reagan Administration fired the PATCO members who went on strike. In the final analysis, PATCO was seeking pay scales equal to that of the pilots. My philosophy pertaining to the on-going dispute between pilots and air traffic controllers is as follows: (Remember, I was on both sides of the fence.) An air traffic controller makes an error, the pilot and his passengers die; however, the controller lives. A pilot makes an error, known as "Pilot Error," the pilot and his passenger's die. You never hear the term "Controller Error", you hear "System Error". Ask yourself: "Who falls the greater distance and who is liable?"

In 1971, PATCO held a first anniversary party of the sickout at the Suffolk House on Lake Ronkonkoma, Long Island. I was invited and, in turn, I sent invitations to Captains Lou Singrossi, Walt Schneider and George Ferdinand, who all lived on Long Island. We had a great time. There was entertainment, great food and drink. I wound up dancing with a voluptuous red head named Kitty. Kitty was quite stunning and had a deep voice that made her very alluring, a la, Gloria Swanson. During a break in the action, there was a stage show, which consisted of a band of female impersonators, including the fabulous "Miss Kitty!" I was quite embarrassed. The Mistress of Ceremonies was a fairly elderly impersonator who I had seen in 1959 at a club in San Francisco named, "Finocchio." This Mistress's claim to fame was a rendition of, "Everything is coming up Roses." She would pull out two bouquets of roses from the sleeves of her dress. You never know.

Three days later, I was flying my usual trip from JFK to Ft. Lauderdale, (FLL). We departed to the northwest on runway 31L, made a left turn and were on radar vectors over the Atlantic Ocean to the southwest. At about thirty-five miles out to sea, Kennedy departure control advised Northeast 831 to contact NY Center on 123.75 Mega Hertz. I contacted NY Center and stated, "NY Center, Northeast 831 is with you on a heading of 220, climbing to flight level 240; NY Center's response "Roger NE 831, Kitty says go direct Sea Isle." Sea Isle is a radio navigational aide on the southern New Jersey coast. The controller issuing the instructions was John Caruso, a good friend and a good controller who recognized my voice and happened to be at the PATCO festivities.

I never had to go back and fly as a flight engineer like the others in my class. Out of my class, there were only two of us, Ed Moore and I. Ed Moore was checked out as a line check captain in his second year with the airline; he is a sharp pilot. In 1967 I went to Boeing 727 first officer training in Boston, I took my initial flight training with Captain Paul Nielsen, who was quite a handsome double for Danny Kaye, the actor/pilot. When I was finished with the initial training, I was sent to Miami to finish up with Captain Clark Willard, Northeast Airlines' chief pilot, aka, "The Channel Fox."

Incidentally, there were two airways, Control 1150 & 1151, which originated at Cape Fear, NC. Control 1150 extended 120 nautical miles east of the United States and terminated at the island of Bimini just east of Miami. This airway was used primarily for traffic in and out of Miami and Ft. Lauderdale. Control 1151, however, extended east of Control 1150 and was the airway that was the gateway to the Caribbean and beyond. The name given these routes was the "Channel." During that part of Clark's career, the majority of his flying was primarily between Miami, his domicile, New York, Boston and Los Angeles. This is how Clark acquired the name " The Channel Fox." My training consisted of flying some instrument approaches, which were accomplished on Grand Bahamas at an airport called West End. There were three of us, Clark, a flight engineer, and me. The object was to bring me up to speed on my first pure jet aircraft. Clark amazed me. He was so precise and exacting with his flying. He flew an aircraft with the precision and perfection of an Arturo Toscannini. Clark gave me some invaluable pointers that stayed with me during the remainder of my flying career.

And now for a flashback, I knew Captain Willard from my crew scheduling days. This brings to mind an incident that occurred on New Year's Eve in 1959. There was a DC6 trip leaving at 21:00 from Idlewild Airport, NY to Miami. Captain Willard was in command and we were missing a flight engineer. When you cannot find an available crewmember for a flight, you have to go in reverse order of seniority according to the Airline Pilots' Association Union contract. It entails taking the published seniority list of the subject airline and working your way from the bottom up until you find someone and assign him the trip. There were only three ways to get out of the trip: 1. Being illegal, which consists of flying over eight hours in a twenty-four hour period. 2. Being sick or on a non-approved medication. 3. Having had a drink of alcohol, within a twenty-four hour period, from bottle to throttle. (This restriction is now eight hours.)

It was about 18:00 I had contacted numerous flight engineers and I got the same answer, "I've had a drink." Remember that it was New Year's Eve. It was about 18:30 and Captain Willard came into crew scheduling, which was located at the hangar and also housed flight control. He asked me if I had covered the flight engineer position yet? When I said that I had not, he asked me whom I had contacted. I gave him the names. He asked me who the most junior man was who I had contacted who had refused the trip. I gave him the name. Captain Willard dialed the phone number. Someone answered the telephone. Captain Willard said, "Is this Sid? This is Captain Willard and I understand that you refused to fly with me to Miami tonight, is that correct?" There was a sustained pause and Captain Willard stated, "I am glad that you reconsidered and I will meet you over at ground operations at 20:00, thank you." He was a *"no nonsense* guy." Incidentally, it took a DC6B four hours and ten minutes to go from Idlewild to Miami; the jet age cut that time in half. The Concorde cut that in half, once again. I had been in the Concorde. It resembled a modern day Pterodactyl. The interior was small and cramped, thus, resembling a Douglas DC9, which was two and two seating. The windows were very small due to pressurization requirements. It was a Mach II aircraft, twice the speed of sound, which is 661 KTS or 761 MPH at Sea Level. It was fast and furious.

Clark is in his nineties now and even as we speak, he is still active in the aviation industry. He holds all kind of aircraft ratings and speed and endurance records on the Convair 880 and the B727 in the 1960s. I just checked my logbook and I started my B727 flight training on October 2, 1967 and completed in Miami on October 18, 1967. I went back to FH227 first officer due to scheduling conflicts. I started to fly B727 First Officer from JFK on December 24, 1967 and remained there until August 29, 1968. I went to FH227 captain training on September 26, 1968 and received my FH227 captain's rating on October 09, 1968. I barely had the required flight time for the rating. Three years with the airline is quite a short time period in which to check out as captain and it is almost unheard of today. Upon completion of captain flight training and passing a rating ride on the Fairchild FH227, it consists of takeoffs, landings, normal and abnormal procedures, engine failures, air maneuvers, instrument approaches and missed approaches. What it amounts to is being hit with anything and everything including the kitchen sink. With all this behind me, I was to fly with a line check airmen for approximately thirty hours to obtain actual experience on actual flights. Many instructor line check airmen are designated by the FAA to instruct pilots who are upgrading to a new piece of equipment. These management pilots are quite impressed with themselves, and revel in the joy of conveying to their students what they know and what the student does not know. This is not always the case; however they usually have a bag of tricks and questions, which are given on a daily basis prior to each training or line-check flight. This situation rarely occurred during my career, but did arise during my first check out on the FH227 in November of 1968. Coincidentally, Northeast Airlines was recovering from a disastrous FH227 crash on Moose Mountain on October 25, 1968 just northeast of Lebanon, NH. It was NE flight 946 from Boston to Montpelier, VT via Lebanon. The captain was quite senior and had flown that area extensively for many years on the DC3. The radio navigational aids were quite outdated and unreliable due to mountainous terrain and mineral deposits. In fact, the altitude restrictions on this non-precision approach were increased at published sunset. This was the case of this approach and crash, which occurred exactly at sunset. To quote Ernest K. Gann, "Fate is the Hunter." I was being line checked subsequent to the crash on the exact route and I could see the wreckage still impaled on Moose Mountain. Needless to say, it had a devastating effect on my performance and me. The line check airman brought up the gory details and findings of the associated crash. By doing so, he put the fear of God in me. Here I am, a brand new captain with minimum time, however, I had a wealth of flight time in the area as a first officer in the DC3 and the FH227 plus I had flown with a group of sharp guys in the New York Base who taught me a great deal. I was not comfortable with this particular line check airman. He was sadistic and reminded me of " Captain Hostile." I requested and received Captain Dick Shreve from Boston. Dick was a fine gentleman and a great instructor pilot. We did a series of trips for one day and he signed me off as completed. Incidentally, Dick's daughter Anita, is the author of numerous best-seller novels, one entitled "A Pilot's Wife." Luckily, I never had to fly with that other instructor for the remainder of my career.

I encountered this type of Napoleonic Complex once again during the latter part of my career. He was a sadistic SOB, a little guy who came out of the military and was quite "Gung Ho." He could make an extended trip across the pond an absolute nightmare. They are sick puppies hell bent on revealing to you and the civilized world that they know more than you will ever know... plus, they have to justify their jobs. In a hundred years from now, it won't mean Diddly Squat.

While in training at Northeast's headquarters in Boston, I recall staying at the Logan Hilton at the airport. One evening after class, I was seated at the restaurant when my eye caught sight of a guy who seemed familiar. I struck up a conversation with him and asked if he was from New York: and he answered in the affirmative, and discovered we were both from Queens and both worked for Northeast Airlines. I asked where, he said LaGuardia. I asked what department, he stated line maintenance. I asked if he knew Joe Tancredi, he replied that Joe was his boss. I asked his name, he said Freddie Favors. I asked if he was in the US Navy; he said yes. I asked if he was in Company 5533; he said yes. I asked if he played in the drum and bugle corps and he said yes. We were in the same company in boot camp. I brought my Navy graduation book from boot camp with all our pictures in it. We became very close friends. Freddy's a great guy. He's retired now and lives in Las Vegas, *Piccolo Mondo*.

I flew captain until January 31, 1969 and then returned to B727 first officer until the merger with Delta Air Lines on August 01, 1972.

As a captain in New York at LaGuardia on the FH227 (Fairchild), I made it a custom to have breakfast with my crew at a diner named the Deer's Head Diner on Astoria Boulevard. One early morning, I was having breakfast with my first officer P.A. Smith and Stewardess Dee Mitchell from Los Angeles. Incidentally, she got fired for converting her uniform skirt to a mini skirt prior to the Yellowbird Campaign. I must admit… she wore it quite well. While engaged in conversation, I noticed a gentleman in the next booth staring at me. I didn't think anything of it at first. However, it started to bother me after a while. A few minutes later, I discovered why. He was my neighbor and good friend, Angelo Cordero, who lived in the next apartment with his wife Marie. Marie's twin sister, Gloria is my Uncle Tom's wife. I hadn't seen Angelo in quite a few years and he was a sight for sore eyes. We hugged and I introduced him to my crew. I include this particular memory at this point in my book because I met with Angelo this very morning (January 08, 2008). It was great seeing him again. Like me, he too was born in Yankee pin stripes. We share heritage and good times. He reminded me of that meeting at the diner so many years ago. I also saw Angelo just recently at my Uncle Tom's funeral, which was quite sad.

I mentioned my first officer P.A. Smith. P.A. was a great guy and a very dedicated first officer who was on probation in his first year. Your first year is the most difficult … the airline can fire you without provocation. P.A., like me, was a low-time civilian pilot. He had a great attitude. We flew the winter of '68 together up and down the Connecticut Valley, which consisted of Hartford, CT, Keene and Lebanon, NH and Montpelier, VT and had a great time. Every month we bid for trips and were awarded a schedule according to seniority.

Like everything else in the airline industry, it is "seniority, seniority, seniority." There were certain individuals you preferred to fly with and naturally there were some you tried to avoid like the plague. Upon terminating the month with me, P.A. received a bid with a captain who had a reputation of being a stickler on procedures and flying by his standards and his standards only. Apparently, during that month, P.A. and this captain went at it and the captain turned him into the chief pilot, which were grounds for dismissal. The chief pilot called Ed Moore and me into his office, knowing we were the last two captains to fly with P.A. and wanted our evaluation. We both gave P.A. a satisfactory report. P.A. completed his probationary period satisfactorily and his thirty plus year career with Northeast/Delta.

There were two FH227 First Officers domiciled in New York who were hired in mid 1968 and were eventually fired prior to completing the first year's probation. One had an attitude problem and the other just did not progress to airline standards. I flew with both of them and I totally agree with Northeast's decision. I will not go into details pertaining to the individual who could not progress, except to say that he was trained on an island where it is always sunny and warm, whereas, in New England it is always diametrically opposed. In 1974, I recall being in Miami at a departure gate awaiting a B727 aircraft, guess who came sauntering up the concourse? The former Northeast Airlines FH227 first officer who couldn't "cut the mustard." He spied me and announced that he was on his way to Winston Salem, NC, the home of Piedmont Airlines and was going to check out as a captain on the FH227. I said, "I hope that you do a better job than you did when you flew for Northeast" enough said.

The individual with the "attitude problem" was a very handsome young man, but he did not excel within the crew concept. For example, he would put abnormal demands upon the flight attendants when their main concern were the passengers. We also had a captain in Boston that required a cup of *"**Demi Tas**"* prior to each flight. The FH227 was a forty-four passenger aircraft with one flight attendant and the average duration of each flight was approximately one hour in length, so, they were quite busy. This first officer known as Les was quite a lady's man and had an ego a mile wide. He lived in an airline ghetto known as Kew

Gardens, Queens, NY otherwise known as "Stew Gardens." Les, was so obnoxious that the flight attendants decided to retaliate. At Christmas time in 1968, they sent Les a gigantic present decorated with fancy wrapping paper, bows and ribbons, along with a Christmas card signed by all the flight attendants "To Les with love." I was flying with Les the day after Christmas when he discovered the beautifully decorated package next to his flight bag in flight operations at LaGuardia. He was quite ecstatic when he spied the package and said to me, "I told you these girls love me and the way I treat them." That being said, Les opened the beautifully decorated package and discovered the gift consisted of cigarette butts, ashes, garbage, food and a garden variety of a conglomeration of household trash… pay back is a bitch. Les had another problem. He'd ask the flight attendants after a series of flights, "Which landing was better, mine or the captain's?" I had a problem with Les landing at Keene, NH, where the runway was quite short and snow coated and one has to apply the brakes aggressively. On this particular flight, Les was so engrossed on making a smooth landing and transition that I had to get on the brakes and stop the aircraft, otherwise we would have run out of runway. In the final analysis, Les was terminated prior to the completion of his probationary period.

Chapter Twelve:

Northeast/ Delta Air Lines Merger, August 01, 1972 to October 02, 1987

A s with any airline merger, the surviving air carrier gains quite substantially; it is the opposite for the air carrier being dissolved. Concerning pilots, the name of the game is seniority, seniority, seniority. This determines flight status, captain vs. first officer vs. flight engineer. Merged pilot seniority lists are usually integrated on a percentage basis. In the Delta-Northeast case, the seniority lists were integrated on a four-and-a half to one ratio, according to the letters of agreement formulated by the ALPA (Airline Pilots Association) representatives in essence meant that there were four and a half Delta pilots implemented into the combined seniority list compared to one Northeast pilot. Don't ask how this was accomplished. Like MONOPLY, the person with the most money and real estate usually wins. This was accomplished through ALPA.

My career started with Delta Air Lines on August 01, 1972 and terminated on my retirement date of May 19, 1996, a total of approximately twenty-four years. Subsequent to the merger, I was based in New York until August 01, 1973 when Delta closed the New York base; a big mistake. I transferred to Miami and commuted to various domiciles for the next twenty-three years of my career. Delta ultimately closed the Miami pilot base and relinquished it to American Airlines, who developed this into an American gateway to the Caribbean and South America.

New York has become one of Delta's biggest moneymakers; it is the gateway from Europe to the United States via the east coast, which Delta acquired through the Pan American acquisition of 1991. Delta reopened the New York base in 1991. This became quite convenient for me with my home in Port Jefferson, NY.

I made it a habit on overnights in cities around the world to visit Catholic Churches and attend Mass. This included The Vatican in Rome when I started to fly international. I happened to be in Rome and at The Vatican when His Holiness, John Paul II returned from the hospital. I photographed him waving to an enormous crowd. I also attended a Mass at Aqueduct Race Track on October 07, 1995 when Pope John Paul II visited New York City. I received the tickets through John Cardinal O'Connor, a personal friend.

I would like to address a few of the Aviation mishaps of the last century. On December 29 1972, a brand new Eastern Airlines Lockheed 1011 departed from New York for Miami. On the approach to Miami, there was a problem with the landing gear warning light system. The crew opted to enter a holding pattern and research the problem, which was an FAA requirement. While in the holding pattern over the Everglades, the three crewmembers were focused on the problem. This was a typical lack of *"cockpit resource management* and *situation awareness."* One of the pilots inadvertently disconnected the autopilot and the aircraft started an undetected very gradual descent to destruction. It was a dark night over the Everglades with no peripheral lights to warn them of the impending disaster. There was no ground proximity warning devices (GPWS) or autopilot disconnect warning horns or lights. In those early days of yesteryear and at 23:42, Eastern Airlines Flight 401 became a statistic. The results of this disaster caused the implementation of the *"ground proximity warning system"* known as GPWS and the autopilot disconnect warning horn and siren. There was a book written, entitled "The Ghost of 401." about Don Repo, the flight engineer. It was quite eerie.

Another disaster changed the entire aviation world forever; this pertained to single-engine aircraft as well as wide-body jumbo jets. The new discovery was a *"microburst."* named by Professor Tetsuya Fujita of the University of Chicago. This discovery stemmed from the crash of Eastern Airlines Flight 66 from New Orleans to New York John F. Kennedy Airport on June 24, 1975 at 16:05. The findings attributed the disaster to "wind shear." The definition of wind shear is as follows: A sudden change in wind direction and velocity, be it vertical or horizontal, within a relatively small area that originates from a thunderstorm. The average person will feel the abnormal cold air preceding the advance of the leading edge of a thunderstorm. The air that you are experiencing originates from the highest strata of the cumulonimbus clouds, some 35,000 feet and above.

I remember that afternoon quite well. I was at home on Long Island and it was a typical hot summer afternoon. Normally at approximately 16:00 cumulonimbus clouds, which are clouds of vertical development, appear on the southwest horizon and move to the northeast. I lived in Port Jefferson and JFK was southwest of my home by approximately forty-five nautical miles. Eastern 66 was on the approach to runway 22L at JFK, which is the primary runway used during summer months, because of the southwesterly winds. Before the crash, a previous aircraft reported wind shear and recommended that there be a runway change to runway 31L or right. There was a previous Eastern flight that executed a "go around" or missed approach, due to an abnormal sink rate and a noticeable drop in indicated air speed. On an approach below one thousand feet above the ground, the flaps are in the landing configuration at thirty degrees, and the landing gear is extended. In this configuration, the aircraft is in a very vulnerable position, especially below three hundred feet above the ground. Eastern flight 66 was about two hundred feet above the ground when it was hit with a vertical gust of approximately twenty-nine feet per second, which would give it 6.90 seconds to analyze the problem, apply maximum power, rotate the aircraft, and "Get the hell out of there…" almost an impossibility under those conditions.

Due to the presence of wind shear, Eastern 66 slammed into the ground over the non-frangible approach light system prior to the runway threshold of runway 22L at JFK; it came to a stop on Rockaway Boulevard, which runs perpendicular to the runway of the intended landing.

Subsequent to this accident, new equipment was incorporated into the aircraft, known as a wind shear alerting system. Revised wind shear recovery procedures were put in place, and are now practiced religiously during simulator training and on pilot proficiency checks, twice a year for a captain.

The National Transportation Safety Board report NTSB-AAR-76-8 stated: " The probable cause of this accident was the aircraft's encounter with adverse winds associated with a very strong thunderstorm located astride the ILS (instrument landing system) localizer course, (azimuth course), which resulted in a high descent rate into the non-frangible approach light towers. The flight crew's delayed recognition and correction of the high descent rate were probably associated with their reliance upon visual clues rather than on flight instrument references. However, the adverse winds might have been too severe for a successful approach and landing even if they had relied upon and responded rapidly to the indications of the flight instruments. Contributing to the accident was the continued use of runway 22L when it should have become evident to both air traffic control personnel and the flight crew that a severe weather hazard existed along the approach path."

Author's Note:

There were no auto land capabilities on the aircraft's auto pilot or flight management system, so pilots were trained at that time that when reaching minimums, normally at 200 feet above the ground, you must have the runway lights or other runway environment in sight, which are the runway threshold lights, the runway and/or the runway markings, to continue the approach to the landing and you have to see one or all of the above and remain visual until touchdown. I think that the crew was perfectly correct to remain visual if the runway environment was in sight, even as sporadic as it was, under those conditions. The only other way was to go back on instruments and execute a "missed approach." The only clue, other than the rate of descent or a decrement of airspeed would have been a sixth sense that you were too low and to get the hell out of there. These evaluations take time and, after all, we are only human. Also, reaction times do differ among humans. This is all based on experience, which comes with age and longevity. A normal glide slope (vertical descent) is normally three degrees, which equates to 756 feet per minute rate of descent at 140 knots or approximately 300 feet per mile. I will re-visit wind shear at length a little later… you'll see how it will hit home.

I continued to fly as first officer on the B727 until 1973, when I checked out as a B727 captain in Miami. Because of the fuel crisis in 1975, my captaincy was short lived. I bid for a Douglas DC10 first officer in Miami and attended DC10 first officer training at American Airlines Flight Academy in Dallas, TX. During the remainder of my career, I would never receive the quality of training that I received at American. During the first training session in the DC10 simulator we were required to practice evacuating the simulator. On my fourth session in this module, "we were flying along in flight," when all of a sudden, the simulator pitched over on its side, putting us on an angle of about forty-five degrees. It was soon apparent that one of the four hydraulic jacks that supported the cockpit of the simulator console came unglued. We had to evacuate the module through an escape hatch. Needless to say, when the training session was over I was "all shook up."

During this time, I maintained a dual qualification, which consisted of a DC10 first officer and a B727 captain. To remain qualified, I was required to make three landings and takeoffs within the previous ninety days on both pieces of equipment plus attend ground school, proficiency checks and line checks within the past year. My qualification was running out on the B-727, which meant that I would have to go out with a line check airman and physically make the required three landings and takeoffs. Miami has an airport just west of Miami International Airport, known as the training and transition airport or TNT, specifically for this purpose.

I was assigned to Captain Dick Houghton and one of my DC3 classmates Captain Chuck Gutierrez. Incidentally, I was best man at Chuck's wedding. We had to go out and execute our three bounces at TNT to maintain our qualification on the B727. We had a great time; we completed it in about an hour. It consisted of one takeoff and two touch and go landing maneuvers, which is a landing and an immediate takeoff without stopping and a landing to a full stop. Then, we changed seats and the other pilot did the same. TNT has one long runway; there is a lighting system that can be activated through a radio frequency at the airport associated with traffic advisories. There is no tower; however, there was a duty fire truck at the airport. In today's world, there are sophisticated simulators, in which one can accomplish the re-qualification process.

I commuted from JFK to Miami every week. On December 06, 1976, I was returning home to New York from Miami on a Delta B727 as a passenger when a passenger collapsed from a heart attack as we were approaching Norfolk, VA. I offered my services as no doctor was on board and I was CPR trained. I teamed up with a student from the University of Miami, a scuba diving instructor and we diverted to Norfolk, VA. We administered CPR for the remainder of the flight and until the paramedics assumed command at the gate in Norfolk. They removed the sixty-one year old man and took him to Norfolk General

Hospital. We then proceeded on our way to New York. The next day I called Norfolk General and was advised that the man had passed away, which saddened me greatly.. Due to my assistance on this flight, I received a **Customer Service Award** from Delta Air Lines for service *"over and above the call of duty "* and two shares of Delta Common Stock.

After flying DC10 first officer and B727 captain, I was transferred to Chicago, on expenses as a B727 captain, so that the Chicago pilots would be relieved of duty to attend B727 flight training in Atlanta. This lasted for about three months. I was then cancelled once more and attended Lockheed L1011 first officer flight training in Atlanta. I flew the L1011 as first officer for six months out of Miami and was awarded a B727 captain's bid in Chicago that lasted until the spring of 1979. I truly enjoyed flying out of Chicago. Everyone there was new on the B727 except us former Northeast pilots. It was a great base with a fine bunch of pilots and a chief pilot named Jack Reeves, who was originally from Chicago C&S (Central and Southern). Jack came to Delta in a merger in the 50s. I had the experience of commanding my first female flight engineer there.

I had the pleasure of flying with a great guy and a fine pilot named Larry Pullen from Houston, TX. We became great friends. Larry is also a professional photographer who gave me permission to use his famous picture of a Delta Air Lines Convair 880 lifting off in Houston for the cover of this book, which incidentally, is quite apropos. In February of 1975, Larry and I were doing a sequence, while flying out of Chicago, which on the second day, originated out of New Orleans with a stop in Memphis, terminating in Detroit for the overnight. The take-off from New Orleans was uneventful. While en-route to Memphis and Detroit we encountered turbulence, as we were traveling behind the back-side of a fast moving cold front which extended from Canada, east of Detroit and to the east of New Orleans. The approach and the landing in Memphis was quite gusty with sporadic heavy rain showers. Upon checking the current weather and forecasts for Detroit, I discovered the rain showers were expected to change to snow in the Ohio Valley, which is quite common at this time of year. I, therefore, requested additional fuel in anticipation of an ATC hold. This turned out to be the proper call on my part, as we experienced an extensive hold in the Detroit area due to weather conditions and snow removal at the airport. Detroit was giving braking action on the landing runway as "poor to nil," which is a "no-no." We held as long as possible and then proceeded to our alternate, which was designated as Dayton, OH. We refueled and returned to Detroit, for another holding session. It was now getting quite late and we as a crew were becoming fatigued. We continued to hold once more under the same conditions. When conditions did not improve, we proceeded back to Dayton, OH and put the airplane to bed for the night. Better safe than sorry.

Two other instances occurred there that were of interest. My philosophy as "pilot in command" was that if there was problems with the aircraft or passenger get the aircraft on the ground ASAP. My passengers' welfare was my prime concern; therefore, when a passenger became ill, I expedited the descent, so that no one could ever come back to me for *"dereliction of duty or poor judgment. "*

Case in point: we had taken off from Chicago O'Hare International Airport, destination Tampa FL, when I was notified that a woman went into labor in the rear lavatory and that no doctor was on board. I immediately requested a diversion to the nearest airport, which was Louisville, KY. We advised the passengers to remain in their seats while the paramedics attended to the patient. The woman was four months pregnant and had suffered a miscarriage and aborted the fetus onboard the aircraft in the aft lavatory. This was a sad outcome; the right decision was made in diverting the aircraft.

On the lighter side, the next scenario is quite hilarious. It is a classic and I was on the third day of a three-day schedule, consisting of a Boston overnight followed by legs from Boston to Baltimore to Atlanta, changing airplanes and flying nonstop to Chicago O'Hare and terminating at my domicile. We were delayed because of foul weather. Upon arrival in Baltimore, I requested additional due to delays in the Atlanta area. I made it a habit to greet the passengers at the forward entrance during board-ing.. We were in the final boarding process and while I was standing in the doorway, a young man walked by me and appeared to have either a knapsack or a parachute on his back. My attention was diverted into the cockpit and when my attention was again focused down the aisle, the passenger was nowhere to be seen. I asked the flight attendant on the jet way if she had seen the young man with the parachute. She replied that she hadn't. I then went to the passenger agent in the terminal and queried him. He stated in the negative also pertaining to the chute. I took it upon myself to check for this mysterious parachute person. I donned my pilot's hat and proceeded down the aisle to the rear air stair door with no luck. I then returned and started forward; just in front of the aft galley on the left side of the aircraft, I noticed the chute under the aisle seat. I asked the young man if that was a parachute under his seat and he said "yes." I stated that due to the D.B. Cooper incident that occurred in 1971, it was against FAA regulations to carry a parachute in the passenger cabin. D.B. Cooper parachuted from the aft air stair door of a B727 over the Pacific Northwest and to this day, he has never been found. The young man stated that he was on his way to Zephyrhills near Tampa, FL for a parachute jump competition and that it was a valuable sport chute. I told the young man that I would gladly store the chute in the cockpit until his arrival in Atlanta. The young man agreed. I nonchalantly threw the chute over my shoulder and proceeded up the aisle toward the cockpit whistling a happy tune a la "***The High and the Mighty.***" The passengers broke out in a fit of laughter that never ceased. Can you imagine seeing your intrepid captain proceeding up the aisle with a chute on his shoulder? Had the media been made aware of this, the newspapers would have had a field day with the headlines akin to "***Airline Captain***

Goes Skydiving." I finally reached the first class section and onboard was a Delta flight crew deadheading (riding as passengers) to New Orleans. The captain laughed so hard that he had tears in his eyes. He finally gained his composure and said, "What's the matter? Is there something that you know that we don't?" Until I retired, if our paths crossed, he would point at me and say, "There's the guy."

On one occasion, I had a Houston overnight. I decided to spend time with my youngest sister Joanne and my three nephews, Gary John, Michael and Andrew. They resided in Spring, TX, which is approximately twenty miles north of Houston. I spent the night there and they accompanied me to the airport the next afternoon. The aircraft for my flight to Atlanta and beyond was delayed some forty-five minutes; so, we decided to sit in the gate area and talk. Upon arrival of the aircraft, I gave them a guided tour of the B727 and said farewell. The flight was uneventful and my landing in Atlanta on runway 26L was absolutely perfection, which in aviation parlance is known as a "Grease-job." One of the contributing factors was that the approach end to runway 26L in Atlanta slopes down and away; thus, the runway is not coming up to meet the aircraft, it is falling away from the descent plane of the aircraft, making it easier during the flare and touch-down portion of the landing. About two months subsequent to the flight, I received a letter of commendation from the C.E.O. of Delta, Mr. David Garrett. Apparently, there was an executive from KLM Royal Dutch Airlines on board, stating that it was the best landing that he had ever experienced. In the letter, the gentleman stated the flight number and that he did not know the captain's name; however, he had heard his nephews call him "Uncle Nick." I guess that it pays to advertise. As they say in the industry, "Any landing that you can walk away from is a good landing.,"

I flew through quite a few severe winter storms while based in Chicago; it goes with the territory. Rough weather has a way of separating the men from the boys. Although I was relatively new as a B727 captain, I had ten years behind me as a Northeast Airlines B727 first officer flying in and out of New England and Montreal during the winter months with a bunch of well-experienced captains who taught me the ropes. On January 12, 1979, Chicago was hit with a snowstorm that lasted two days and deposited twenty inches of newly driven snow on top of ten inches from a previous storm, crippling air travel in and out of Chicago for the next five days. This storm was a classic example of the lake effect; whereby a cold front associated with a low-pressure area that originated in Siberia, Russia, would gain strength and moisture traversing through northern Canada, across the Great Lakes into the northern United States. On the sixth day, I was called out to do a round trip to Atlanta and transport stranded flight crews who were unable to return to base. The takeoff and trip to Atlanta was uneventful except for the poor conditions of the taxiways and associated runways. On our return trip we had, three displaced crews deadheaded to O'Hare with us. I requested extra fuel anticipating a lengthy hold in the Chicago area, which did indeed come to pass. Upon arrival in the terminal area, we were advised that the only runway available was 32L. It was normally 11,000 foot long; however, the encrusted ice and hard packed snow reduced the runway length to only 6,000 feet available. My major concern was to have the 152,000-pound aircraft completely stopped prior to entering the ice and snow. If we hit this area with any form of forward speed, we would shear off the nose gear. I discussed this approach with both my pilots and the flight attendants. I stated that, depending on the braking action on the runway, I would apply the brakes as required and utilize maximum reverse thrust from the three engines, so that we would be completely stopped prior to taxing into the rutted portion of the runway. I planned to touch down at the beginning of the exposed tarmac and apply maximum braking. The four brakes on the four main gear wheels of the B727 were equipped with anti-skid devices so that no wheels would lock up and blow tires in the event of hydroplaning. I touched down and simultaneously applied near maximum braking and maximum reverse thrust on the engines as soon as the nose gear was on the runway. There were some patches of ice and snow; however, the applied braking was quite effective considering runway conditions. I had the aircraft well under control and completely stopped prior to the rutted area. We had to travel through this area to get to a taxiway that would take us to the terminal and gate. We arrived at the gate some thirty minutes later due to the horrendous conditions on the tarmac. It took an additional ten minutes to properly position the jet-way, so that the entrance door could be opened properly. When the entrance door was finally opened, I stood at the door to greet the passengers as they departed. One of the passengers deplaning from the first class section was a senior captain from the Chicago domicile who had a reputation for being a worrier. On his way out, he berated me in front of my passengers for applying excessive braking. Doing so in front of passengers is contrary to etiquette and protocol. I stated that I wanted to meet with him and discuss this further in the presence of the Chicago chief pilot. I read him the riot act and stated how dare he second-guess my decisions while he was sitting in the comfort of a first class seat without the full knowledge of the environment and its potential ramifications. I also stated that I had been flying the B727 since 1967 and knew the capabilities of this aircraft far better than he, noting that this was his first winter on this aircraft. Had he been flying the aircraft, I'm sure he would have diverted and changed his diaper. In conclusion, what he did and said was contrary to everything that has ever been written on crew resources management. It equates to pulling the trigger on a loaded weapon without aiming at the target and shooting ones self in the foot.

Many of us New York pilots bid Chicago in order to be as close to New York as possible. Of course the Boston Domicile is closest and more desirable. Boston is a very senior former Northeast Airlines base. In Chicago, we were biding our time until we could gain enough seniority to fly out of Boston. I commuted between New York and Chicago via

American Airlines or United Air Lines. There was service every hour to Chicago and the discount fares were quite cheap back then. I commuted with my buddy George Ferdinand who was a great guy to fly with and a true friend. George and I did quite a few trips together as we were both on reserve. We were assigned a trip on the B727 with a brand new flight engineer fresh out of the Air Force, who I called "Tom Terrific," for obvious reasons. The trip consisted of a three days encompassing the Ohio Valley. We started out of Chicago, flew to Cincinnati, Louisville, Atlanta and on to Miami. There was a front in the Ohio Valley with some low level thunderstorms at 17,000 feet and no threat to our flight schedule. I flew the Cincinnati to Louisville leg; we climbed through some turbulence and broke out on top at 24,000. The trip to Louisville was relatively short, therefore we had to let down into some light to moderate turbulence. No big deal if you slow to turbulence penetration speed of M.78/280 knots. On descent we encountered some unexpected turbulence, as our radar was not picking up these fairly weak low-level turbulent cells. We encountered some moderate rain, which would scare the living daylights out of a new kid on the block. This was the case with our new engineer, Tom. I do not know what he flew in the US Air Force, but he looked a little pale and had his eyes glued to the engineer's panel. We did get bounced around due to malfunctioning radar. To cut to the chase, we got to Miami and checked into the hotel and Tom's room was next to mine. As I was to opening my door and entering my room for a good night's sleep, Tom says, "Can I ask you a question?" I said, "Sure what is on your mind?" He asked me why did I take off from Cincinnati? I answered, "As captain of this aircraft and based on my extensive experience and the fact that there were no thunderstorms reported at the airport and that the storms were low level. Further, based upon my dedication to Delta Air Lines and in the interest of my passengers, I felt sure I would successfully complete my mission and earn my pay…which I did." I continued with: "How dare you question my decisions!" I stated that when we returned to our home base we should sit down with the chief pilot and the union official and thrash out his concerns pertaining to my decision to complete the flight. We had no idea that the Radar would not interrogate the low level cells. Later, I discovered that Tom Terrific decided to become a union official and duck his responsibilities as an airline pilot, sharp-shooting the union agreement and flying a union desk. "To each his own."

Elsewhere in this book, I will go into the paranoia that sets in when an individual passenger steps foot on an aircraft and verbally displays his/her lack of knowledge pertaining to the science of aerodynamics. Such is the case of the next scenario. I was doing a B727 trip from Cincinnati to Philadelphia. It was late at night and the weather was horrible. The air was quite turbulent and it was snowing in the destination area. FYI: there is no such thing as an ***"Air Pocket,"*** which is merely a colloquial expression. Basically, an "Air Pocket" is a dis-laminar flow of air, occurring when two different strata of air cross each other at opposing angles, which, in turn, causes turbulence. I tried to find a suitable altitude but to no avail. I went from 37,000 feet down to 24,000 feet plus every altitude in between. The duration of the flight was one hour and ten minutes without any smooth air. The approach in the snowstorm was quite turbulent especially down close to the ground. The landing itself was good, but on touchdown the landing roll was turbulent due to crosswinds. It took us some twenty minutes to taxi to the gate as many taxiways were closed, plus another ten minutes to position the jet-way. The door finally opened and the passengers deplaned and I was glad that this trip was over. Many passengers thanked me for getting them there safely, however, one of those paranoid passengers said, "May I ask you a question? " I respectfully stated, "What is that, sir?" He asked, "Are you just learning how to fly." I had to control myself and maintain my professionalism. However, I always considered the source. At that point in time, I had been a Pilot in Command on the B727 for eighteen years.

Another incident occurred on a flight from Tampa to Chicago. We were two hours late departing Tampa International Airport, plus another hour before we were airborne due to air traffic control delays landing at O'Hare. One hour into the flight, the first class flight attendant stated that there was an elderly lady in first class who was acting up and creating havoc. She was calling the young lady along side of her every expletive in the book, for no apparent reason. I told the flight attendant to inform her that it is a violation of Federal Air Regulations to interfere with the operation of an aircraft either on the ground or in the air and that this behavior is punishable by a fine and/or imprisonment. I told the flight attendant to tell her to govern herself accordingly and ask her name and original seat assignment. I also stated that if she did not cease and desist I would send the flight engineer back to talk to her and would advise the authorities to meet the aircraft on arrival at O'Hare. Half an hour went by before the flight attendant reappeared in the cockpit and said that the elderly woman was threatening to take off her clothes. I sent the flight engineer back to evaluate the situation and to advise her that the next person she would have to confront would be the captain and she would have to suffer the consequences. The flight engineer returned reporting that she would not cooperate with the crew's requests whatever. When a crewmember leaves the cockpit with the aircraft above 24,000 feet, the remaining pilot has to don an oxygen mask until that person returns; this is a Federal Air Regulation. I left the cockpit and approached the elderly woman. I presented her with my business card and asked, "May I help you?" She was completely incoherent. I requested that if she didn't stop harassing the passengers and flight attendants that I would have no choice but to put the aircraft down and have the authorities remove her from the aircraft. With that she asked, "Where's the door? I'll get out right now." I returned to the cockpit and instructed the flight engineer to contact the company and have the O'Hare passenger service supervisor and airport police meet the aircraft on arrival. We landed and proceeded to the gate. The front cabin door opened and a group of people were waiting for this passenger. They came aboard to confront the woman and escort her off the airplane. The flight attendant introduced me to the husband. I stated that his wife refused to give her name and as a formality we needed the name for the required reports. With that, the husband stated, "Well if she will not give her name, neither will I." I summoned a policeman and stated, "Officer, this gentleman will not cooperate with the authorities." The authorities and the Delta representatives escorted everyone concerned away. Sometime in 2003, I learned that the male involved was instrumental in the infamous John Wayne Gacey Murder Trial in Cook County, IL.

I had the opportunity to fly with my first African-American first officer. His name was Fred Boone. He was an Air Force pilot… a great pilot and a fun guy. We did a number of trips together and kept in touch during my career. Fred eventually became the Project Manager for Delta Air Lines Lockheed L1011 Program, a highly prestigious position. You had to know the designated aircraft better than anyone else on the property.

My tour of duty in Chicago ended in June of 1979. Subsequently, I received a B727 captain's bid in Boston, which made my commute from Long Island to Boston considerably easier and less costly. I enjoyed Boston very much. This was the last stronghold of former Northeast pilots. The chief pilot's office had some great people including Tom Kirby, with whom I flew on the L1011 in Miami, Roger Green and Dave Bushey who became Senior Vice President of Flight Operations with Delta and Jet Blue. I understand that Dave was a tank commander in the US Army and flew for Pilgrim Airlines. The chief pilot's secretary was Janet Jameson. She ran the office and is a fine lady.

My commuting consisted of going to LaGuardia and catching the Eastern or the American shuttle or possibly a flight from McArthur Airport at Islip, Long Island, which was an up and coming airport. I tried to get airline service into Islip many years ago, without success. On many occasions when I would arrive late at night in Boston, I had to stay overnight and catch a nap in the crew lounge on a reclining chair. On one occasion, I had to take Amtrak to Boston, a total of five hours on the train to cover a trip. On another occasion, I arrived late on a Saturday night and the first Eastern shuttle to NY left at 08:30. I arrived there at 07:30 and was sitting at the gate when a 5'2" man with gray hair who was a chain smoker wearing a white Loden coat appeared; it was Leonard Bernstein, the world famous composer/conductor. He was carrying a brief case, which contained the scores of his performance at the Boston Symphony the night before. Leonard was there with his daughter and granddaughter. Being a musician and a devotee of classical music, I listened very intently to their conversation. Leonard was serenading his granddaughter to the melodic sounds of Beethoven's "Fur Elise," which is one of the basics of classical piano and one of my favorites, as well as, my pianist/nephew Michael Elf's favorites.

While flying out of Boston, I was scheduled to do a trip from Boston to Newark then on to Atlanta. The trip to Newark was uneventful. Prior to our departure from Newark, I was standing at the forward entry door and greeting the passengers. Before my eyes appeared an absolutely stunning young lady in her mid-twenties with the most engaging smile I have ever seen. She had the looks and complexion of a Dresden Doll. I could not keep my eyes from looking at this goddess quality beauty. My eyes followed her down the aisle into tourist class and finally to her seat. The front entrance door was closed and we took off on runway 22R in Newark for Atlanta. Upon reaching our cruising altitude I turned off the seatbelt sign and there was an immediate knock on the cockpit door. The engineer opened the door and there appeared a flight attendant who advised us that one of the passengers left her purse in the passenger lounge in Newark and asked if we would have Delta check to see if it was found. We contacted the company via radio and advised them of the lost purse. I told the flight attendant that the company was notified and that it would take approximately fifteen minutes to receive an answer. We received a cell call from the company, in essence, is a bell-type notification system, that the purse was located and asked where the person wanted it sent? This message was relayed to the passenger and a reply was brought forward to send to the company. The message consisted of the following, "Please send my purse to Ms. Sandra Smith, Bunny Mother, care of the Playboy Mansion, McAfee, NJ. Thank you, Miss Patricia Browning." Upon arrival in Atlanta, I was standing in the doorway, naturally, to gain another look at this beautiful creature. As she approached, I knew it was she who misplaced the purse and stated without thinking, "Are you the dumb bunny who left her purse in Newark?" She just smiled brightly and answered politely, "Yes, and I resemble that remark." She then departed my world, never to be seen by me again.

In January of 1980, I decided to purchase a single engine aircraft to commute between Long Island and Boston after flying with First Officer John Duel from Orient Point, NY to Norwood, MA. John pioneered this form of commutation, a typical modus operandi for airline pilots. It is a way of getting to work at your convenience. There are always great concerns pertaining to weather, winds and icing conditions especially in the Northeast area of the country. I did this for three years and at times, it became very arduous. Need I say more? I developed a system to remove ice on the aircraft in preparation for my trip from Boston to Islip, NY. This system incorporated a giant three-gallon pump sprayer, which contained ethylene glycol and water; the same ingredients are used by the airlines and as anti-freeze in an automobile radiator. I also had scrapers, brooms and a hose extension to the tail pipe of my big Mercury automobile to supply heat to the oil in the engine compartment. I used synthetic aviation oil, known as Aero Shell, which was specifically used for operation in very cold winter temperatures.

I would complete my schedule in Boston at 21:30 and leave Logan Airport via auto to Norwood, MA some twenty-five miles southwest of Boston. I would preflight my Mooney 20F, file a flight plan, receive a clearance and finally fly to Islip. The trip to Islip was 133.6 nautical miles, which took an hour. I had to secure the aircraft and then drive another twenty-five minutes to my home in Middle Island, NY. If I arrived home by 01:00, I was lucky and quite fatigued, even though, I was in my early forties at that time.

In March of 1982, I was flying with a flight engineer who lived in New London CT, which was on my way to Boston. I arranged to pick him up and fly on to Boston. We were scheduled to complete a four-day trip and return at the customary 21:30 on the fourth day. The weather was a little testy on the fourth day. Upon checking the weather and filing an IFR (Instrument Flight Rules) flight plan, I discovered that there was a fast moving cold front approaching Boston that would move from the northwest to the southeast. This is typical of cold fronts in the Northern Hemisphere. This would affect our trip to New London and eventually Islip, NY. We decided to wait it out at Norwood until the cold front passed through New London. There were heavy rains, strong northwesterly winds and thunderstorms associated with the cold frontal passage. We decided to take a nap in the car, as we had been up all day and it was now approaching midnight. We finally took off around 01:00 and the eighty-two nautical mile flight to New London was uneventful. I then took off VFR (Visual Flight Rules) to Islip, NY, which was fifty-one nautical miles in distance. I flew southwest along the Connecticut shoreline until the Millstone nuclear power plant and climbed to 5,000 feet for the seven nautical mile crossing of Long Island Sound to Orient Point via Plum Island. This would enable me to glide to a landing on a beach at Orient Point in the event of an engine failure.

This leg of the trip was longer than normal because of the abnormal head winds encountered behind the cold front, which switched from southwest to northwest. It took me forty-five minutes to travel the distance to Islip. I contacted Islip fight service, which is an advisory service since the tower was closed. The air traffic control towers at smaller airports normally close at 22:00. Islip flight service advised me that the runway lighting system was set on runway 24, which is south-west, prior to shutting down the tower. Landing on another runway without the lighting is a *"no-no."* The present winds were reported as three hundred thirty degrees magnetic at twenty-five knots gusting to forty-five knots, well above the maximum crosswind component of the aircraft ninety degrees to the runway. To calculate the winds, the FAA and the airlines state that you take one-half the prevailing wind and the entire gust. One half of twenty-five equals twelve and one half, plus all the gust, which was from twenty-five to forty-five knots or twenty knots. Therefore, I had twelve and one half knots plus twenty knots, or a grand total of thirty-two and one half knot crosswind, which was well beyond the crosswind capability of the Mooney aircraft of 15 knots perpendicular to the runway. The nearest alternate airport was Kennedy Airport, forty-five miles west of Islip. Light single-engine aircraft were not permitted to land there. Since the air traffic control tower was closed, the runway lights remained on runway 24 instead of runway 33. Runway 33 would have given me a direct head wind and no crosswind condition. There were no procedures in the aircraft manual to cover a condition as serious as this. I had to rely on my seventeen years as an airline pilot and the numerous hours of training to modify procedures for this crosswind situation. The Mooney is a strong, well-built aircraft. The normal approach speed was seventy knots with full flaps. In this case, I decided on no flaps and an approach speed of one hundred and ten knots and no flare upon landing. The flare is accomplished by applying backpressure on the control wheel, just prior to touchdown that arrests the decent rate of the aircraft by deflecting the elevator flight control on the tail. In this situation, I flew the aircraft on to the runway without arresting the rate of decent, or sink rate. On the approach, I held thirty-degrees of crab into the wind. This had to be done by deflecting the nose of the aircraft into the wind, so that the track across the ground was an extension of the centerline of the runway. The crab had to be taken out just prior to landing. To do this, I had to coordinate the reduction of the crab (the angle created by the amount of correction needed into the wind to maintain a desired path across the ground) by increasing the bank angle into the wind. In doing so, I had to land on one wheel in a slight nose high attitude, so that I would land on the main wheels and not on the nose wheel that would have been a disaster. During this maneuver which requires perfect coordination of ailerons, rudder and elevator, I ran out of aileron and rudder travel exactly at touchdown. This meant that I would have landed with a sideward motion of a downwind movement. However, I lucked out that this occurred just as I touched down. Upon touching down, I reduced the throttle to idle and held the aileron and rudder inputs as they were on touchdown, making sure that the aircraft settled to the ground when it was good and ready to quit flying. I had a 6000' x 150' wide concrete runway to stop this aircraft. I did not touch a thing until we stopped our forward journey. If I attempted to apply power to taxi, the airplane would have jumped into the air because the wind was above the stall speed of the aircraft. I shut down the engine, attached the tow bar and tied it down to the nearest available area on the ramp.

Needless to say this was an exhibit of superior airmanship on my part, or maybe just pure luck. Subsequent to that episode, I decided to commute to Boston and return on Business Express, a Delta Connection carrier.

I did some charter work for some friends, especially Rudy Then, a great friend who I miss dearly; Rudy was a US Navy pilot during the Korean War. I flew charters throughout the Northeast area, Pennsylvania, Maine and West Virginia. I also took friends on sightseeing trips over New York City at night. I even took a fighter named Gerry Cooney, a heavyweight contender for the title, to the Concord Hotel in the Cats-kills, which was his training camp. Eventually, Larry Holmes cleaned his clock and his career.

I had the distinct pleasure of giving my nephew and godson, Gary John, his first ride in my Mooney 20F in 1981. That one-hour ride became the turning point in his life, as was the 1939 New York World's Fair in mine. I will elaborate on this at the end of this journey. I sold the aircraft in 1982. Subsequently, the aircraft has tripled in price even now with aviation fuel at five dollars a gallon plus.

The stress associated with being an airline pilot, so frequently being away from home, enduring training requirements, the physical and mental drain, etc. takes an enormous toll on a family and a marriage. It takes a great amount of work and dedication, on the part of all family members to make the relationship among husband, wife and children survive.

In 1984, my wife and I decided to build a home on Tierra Verde, south of St. Petersburg, FL and I planned to commute and fly out of Atlanta. This endeavor turned out to be a total disaster. The alleged builder used his brother's license to build a home plagued with substandard materials, construction techniques and lack of inspections by Pinellas County. The house settled severely. It ultimately went to trial. The judge declared a mistrial and the builder walked *"Scot Free."* In October of 1987, I sold the home for the price of the land, went back to New York, transferred back to Boston from Atlanta on the B727, and built a home in Port Jefferson, NY.

Tierra Verde is an island in the Gulf of Mexico that is situated just south of St. Petersburg, FL and just northwest of the ultra modern Skyway Bridge. The Spanish originally settled the island and built a fort at the southern tip of the island named Fort Desoto, in honor of the Spanish explorer Hernando Desoto. My leisure time consisted of sailing my thirty-eight foot Irwin sloop, which I had transported from Long

Island Sound to a canal at the back of my new home. Tierra Verde was chosen for the movies "Cocoon" and "Summer Rental." Ron Howard, little Opie from the Andy Griffin Show, directed "Cocoon." During the filming of the movie, Ron rented a house two blocks from mine. The film "Summer Rental" with John Candy and Richard Crenna was filmed right in my back yard and if you look very carefully, you will see my sloop in the background. I frequented a jazz club on Treasure Island that was named "Green Streets." To get to Tierra Verde, you had to cross two bridges. The first bridge took you from St. Petersburg on to the island and terminated at Fort Desoto, by traveling on the Pinellas Bay-way. The second bridge was a relatively small bridge that connected the eastern portion of the island with the outside world. I crossed the bridge and drove two blocks, turned left and would proceed to the home that I had built at 115 9th Street East. When I first moved there, I noticed a home that resembled a giant Swiss Chalet. It was a symmetrical two family, two-story home that was owned and occupied by the Swedish singing group, ABBA. ABBA represents the first initials of the two husbands and two wives comprising the group. I often drove by their home and observed the foursome playing touch football on the street in front of their home. They were two very handsome couples that required their privacy, which we as neighbors, highly respected.

Phil the Imposter

One Sunday afternoon, while attending a jazz concert at Green Streets, I met a gentleman named Phil who hailed from Indiana. He claimed he flew F4's for the US Air Force in Viet Nam with the infamous River Rats and B727's for Northwest Airlines. We became quite friendly; but when I attempted to glean information on his service record or his tenure with Northwest, he asked, "Are you on a fishing expedition?" Phil even showed me a picture of himself in an airline uniform. One time I asked him a question about the hydraulic brake system pertaining to the B727 and he freaked out on me. There are two systems that power the hydraulic fluid to the brakes: one is the engine driven pumps, known as the "A" system and then there is the back-up electric system, known as the "B" system. The B system powered the brakes. There was a way to remember the components of the "B" system and that was the expression, "Brake in upstairs." This equates to the main brakes, inboard flight spoilers on the wings, the upper rudder and finally the rear aft air stairs. Everything else hydraulically on the aircraft was powered by the "A" system. Phil refused and was unable to provide me with the answer. I started to get skeptical of Phil and his flying machines. I examined the studio photo of him in uniform and discovered that it was not the Northwest emblem on his captain's hat. In a casual discussion, he stated that he had to retire from Northwest due to a heart problem. I asked him if he was on disability with the airline or did he have it from ALPA (Air Line Pilots Association Union), he was unable to give me the answer. Phil also stated (the clincher that he was not what he appeared to be) that due to the heart problem, the FAA took away his ATP (Air Transport Pilot) flight rating, which is required to fly as a captain. Phil claimed that he was left with just a private pilot's license. This is where he fouled up. The only way the ratings may be removed from your license is by a pilot being found guilty of causing an accident (pilot error) or a major crime. You never lose your pilot's ratings associated with an illness; you lose your ability to maintain a medical certificate. Armed with this information, I wrote to Northwest Airlines requesting information on Phil's employment. I received a letter in return that Phil never was employed by Northwest in any capacity whatsoever. I even took the investigation one step further. I contacted one of my first officers in Chicago who was in charge of the Midwest Chapter of the " River Rats," seeing that Phil was from Indiana and would have been a member. I received a letter from Ken Thomas that he never heard of him. Phil had all the accoutrements of an airline pilot. For example, he had a uniform, a flight bag and even an honorary membership in ALPA (Air Line Pilots Association). He was well read on the subjects, but not totally. I have lost track of Phil; however, I still have the feeling that he continues to masquerade as an airline pilot somewhere out there... a la Frank Abagnale, Jr, who carried out his charade quite successfully in the 1960s. There was a movie made with Leonardo DiCaprio, called "Catch Me If You Can." portraying Frank. During the aftermath of 9/11, I was tempted to have the FBI look into Phil's portrayal as an airline pilot. I decided that he was what my father used to say was " A Has Been That Never Was."

While flying out of Atlanta and commuting to Tampa, I had three occasions to transport Jimmy and/or Roslyn Carter on my aircraft. The first occasion was in Jackson, MS and I was scheduled to proceed to Atlanta non-stop. Onboard was Roslyn Carter with Secret Service... she was on a book signing tour. We were informed that there would be a forty-five minute delay due to traffic saturation in the Atlanta area. My air traffic controller expertise became quite valuable. I had my flight engineer call the company and advise ATC that we had Mrs. Carter and the Secret Service onboard and requested special handling. The delay was rescinded and we were expedited into Atlanta, post haste. It pays to know someone.

The second occasion with the Carters originated in New York and terminated in Tampa. Jimmy and Roslyn were in New York after visiting with Amy at Brown University in Rhode Island. He came to the cockpit of the B727 and chatted with us for about ten minutes. We flew to Atlanta and completed my day's work.

The third encounter occurred after the termination of that flight in Atlanta. I was meeting my wife in Atlanta and we were to travel together to Tampa and on to our home on Tierra Verde. The aircraft to Tampa was a B757 and we were flying in a status called "space available," we were last to board. However, we received the first two seats, 1D, and

1E, on the right side of the aircraft in first class. We got settled and noticed this gigantic man sitting across the aisle from us. He was young, very well dressed and had a military crew cut. As the flight was closed out and the door was shut, this man talked to something in his right sleeve; he was also wearing an earpiece. This continued as the flight took off for Tampa. This fellow was so huge that we could not see if there was someone sitting beside him. We noticed that there was a woman sitting directly behind him who was talking to her sleeve. We thought it was weird; but went about our own business. On one occasion, the man crossed his legs and exposed a gun in a holster attached to his right leg. About halfway through the one hour and twenty minute flight, the woman sitting next to the giant got up to go to the lavatory... low and behold it was Roslyn Carter. Mrs. Carter recognized me from her previous flight and said "Hello." I introduced her to my wife. She and the female Secret Service agent proceeded to the forward lavatory. It appeared now that all the pieces to this intriguing puzzle finally came together. We arrived in Tampa and said our goodbyes to Roslyn. Jimmy went back to Plains and Roslyn was going to a health spa in Safety Harbor, FL. We departed the terminal via an employee elevator that took us under the terminal. While leaving the elevator, we saw three black limousines. I was approached by one of Delta's ground personnel who said that the area was crawling with Secret Service agents. I told him that I was aware. Our car was parked in the employees' lot about a mile and a half from the terminal. As we were walking the three limos passed us on the service road and as the last one went by, we saw Roslyn Carter waving to us.

During my career, I had the opportunity to have many celebrities on-board my aircraft. The first one as captain was during my Fairchild days with Northeast Airlines and actor Robert Ryan accompanied me from LaGuardia to Lebanon, NH. He was a graduate of Dartmouth College, in Hanover/White River Junction, NH. I had Tony Bennett on a flight from Houston to JFK. As I was doing my preflight check list on a DC10 as first officer, I happened to turn around to check a circuit panel and there in the doorway was Mr. B. Without batting an eye, I said in Italian, "Hey Piasano, come stai"? Which means, "Hey brother, how are you?" He replied, "Molto bene, molto bene," or "Very good, very good." Tony's brother had opened an Italian restaurant in the Galleria in Houston and named it "Papa DeBenedetto's." On a B767 from Atlanta to Los Angeles, we were instructed to delay the flight at the gate for singer Lionel Richie. His father had passed away in Alabama and he was attending the funeral. We were delayed fifteen minutes. He came up and personally thanked the crew for holding the flight, a nice gesture. I transported Luciano Pavarotti from Rome to JFK and Pete Sampras from Paris to JFK, after the Paris Open Tennis Tournament. I also flew Elke Sommer, Shirley Maclaine and Nipsy Russell, just to name a few.

In March of 1985, I was on a three-day trip with an overnight in Jacksonville, FL on the second night. We were scheduled to fly from Jacksonville to New York's LaGuardia and then on to Atlanta, after which I planned to proceed home to Tierra Verde, FL. We reported to the airport in Jacksonville and discovered that our aircraft would be delayed one hour due to weather and air traffic. I decided to go up to the gate and wait out the delay there. Upon arrival at the gate, a well-dressed middle-aged man approached and inquired as to the time of arrival of the inbound aircraft. When asked his final destination, he answered "New York." We then engaged in quite a fine conversation. He was from Upper Brookville, which I knew to be quite an affluent neighborhood. The man was dressed in a blue blazer with an emblem below his left pocket. I inquired as to the origin of the emblem. He said it was the logo of one of his companies and it was from White Stack Tugboats based in Charleston, SC. I mentioned that my sister was married to Eugene F. Moran III of Moran Tugs in New York. He told me that he knew the Morans. His name was Bart Turacamo. The moment I heard his name, I had a flashback to my childhood and my maternal grandfather, Giuseppi Macaluso and the 1940s. I told him that my grandfather worked for Turacamo Paving, Inc. in the 30s, 40s, and 50s. His father started the company upon his arrival in America from Italy. When he learned my grandfather was Giuseppi Macaluso, he almost fainted. My grandfather used to babysit for him as a child! The elderly man who was accompanying him worked with my grandfather constructing the major roadway system in New York City in the 1930s. Once again " *It's a small world after all.*" I was so elated that this gentleman knew and respected my grandfather. God bless my Italian-American Heritage.

The catering division of Delta Air Lines approved a new menu for the first class cuisine on domestic flights. One of the additions was a new salad dressing known as "poppy seed vinaigrette." At this point in time, drug testing came into existence for pilots and flight attendants. Numerous over-the-counter drugs when taken caused the tested individual to give what is known as a "false positive" test. Cough medicine, antihistamines, etc could cause this. It was also known that "poppy seed dressing" would give a false positive indication of Opium. We started a campaign to have this salad dressing removed from the menu. It was taken to Mr. Ron Allen, the CEO of Delta Air Lines. Finally, the powers that be saw the light and had it removed. Problem solved

Another experience I wish to relate occurred on August 02, 1985… the crash of Delta Flight 191, an L1011 from Ft. Lauderdale to Los Angeles via Dallas, TX. This incident was especially sad for me… it involved a personal friend. I was at my home in Tierra Verde, FL having just finished dinner. It was 19:30. During the regularly scheduled program "Jeopardy," the network interrupted with the horrific news of the disaster. I immediately called crew scheduling in Atlanta and spoke to Doris Davidson, the supervisor on duty. She advised me that the captain was Ted Connors, age fifty-seven, whom I had known since 1957, from my days as a passenger service agent with Northeast Airlines at LaGuardia. Ted was a Convair 240 captain residing on Long Island at that time. Ted was a sharp boy, a great pilot, and a dear friend. Ted and his wife Cathy was the only Northeast Airline crew to visit the exotic island of Cuba in the 1960s, compliments of a skyjacker and Fidel Castro. I used to push a ramp up to his airplane at LaGuardia and he always had a big Irish smile on his good-looking face. Ted was very interested in my progress as a fledgling pilot.

I stayed very close to the NTSB (National Transportation Safety Board) investigation and their eventual findings. In my estimation, Ted did exactly what he was trained to do. He was a victim of circumstances. The accident occurred at 18:05.57 on August 02, 1985 according to the flight/voice recorder.

The following excerpts come from the NTSB Identification DCA85AA031 report.

> "Possible scattered thunderstorms were forecast & during arrival, several cells were developing in the area. Delta 191 was vectored around a large cell, then was sequenced behind other aircraft & cleared for an ILS runway 17L approach. The flight crew & several proceeding crews saw lightning in a cell north of the airport, but continued without reporting it. On the approach, Delta 191 encountered a microburst while passing under the cell. Initially, the first officer, who was flying the aircraft, retarded the throttles in a headwind. The aircraft then encountered approximately 73 knots of wind shear, up/downdrafts, vortex flow & a tailwind. Go-around power was applied, but the aircraft struck the ground approximately 6300 feet north of runway 17L, hit a car and both water tanks, broke apart and burned. Investigation revealed that between 1752 & 1800 central daylight time, the thunderstorm cell grew from VIP Level 1 to VIP Level 4. A center

weather service unit meteorologist was on duty, but not at the radar position at that time & didn't observe the cell growth. Captain's decision to continue approach didn't comply with Delta's weather avoidance procedures. There was a lack of specific guidance & training for avoiding and escaping low altitude wind shear."

There were some things missing in this report; however, the pilots in the industry, especially the Delta Air Lines pilots, knew these facts. The major factor was that the meteorologist on duty was out having dinner, and there was no replacement. Thus, no one discovered the development of this horrendous ***Thunderstorm* And *Microburst*.**

When I worked for the FAA as an air traffic controller in New York Center, we would eat at the scope or starve because there were no replacements and no time for a break. A vacant radar position on that day and time was a ***"DISASTEROUS MISTAKE"*** on the part of the FAA; because as every pilot and controller knows, this is the time of day when cumulonimbus (thunderstorms) are at their severest and require constant monitoring. Only the FAA air traffic control tower has the authority to stop approaches or change runways of the landing of air traffic. This is what should have been done instead of the pilot executing an attempted go around or missed approach. Ted was a victim of circumstances… he was too low and too late. As usual, it was attributed to ***"Pilot Error"*** and not ***System Error."*** The FAA is responsible for establishing training curriculum and approving procedures pertaining to situations like this.

According to what I have also heard from survivors is that the aircraft was forced down to the ground by the horrific microburst. It landed intact and was considered a survivable hard landing a mile short of the runway. After touchdown the left engine on the wing hit an automobile on the roadway just north of the runway. The impact with the automobile caused the left engine to separate from the wing assembly, causing the main body of the aircraft to pivot to the left, setting up a collision course with the two gigantic water tanks parallel to the threshold of runway 17L. (That is no place to position water tanks.) This caused the horrific explosion and inevitable disaster. On numerous occasions, subsequent to the disaster, I flew that approach to runway 17L, saw those two water tanks and would get quite upset. God rest their souls.

On January 27 1986, my wife and I left our home on Tierra Verde for a family reunion in Dayton, OH via Tampa, Atlanta, and Dayton. We arrived in Atlanta at 10:35 and had a two-hour wait in Atlanta for the Atlanta to Dayton flight. We were sitting in concourse A at the departure gate of A19 when an old friend named Earl Jenkins approached me. He was an operations agent who I knew from Jackson, MS. Earl advised me that at 11:39.13 the shuttle Challenger exploded on takeoff from Cape Canaveral, FL. We immediately went to one of the CNN monitors located throughout the airport and viewed the horrific explosion of the shuttle.

While living in Tierra Verde, FL, I was invited to my cousin Joe Zagorski's daughter, Carole Anne's wedding in New York. We departed Tampa International Airport for LaGuardia on April 02, 1987 and would attend the wedding on April 03, 1987. Upon checking in at the ticket counter, I was made aware that I would be sitting next to Dwight Gooden, the New York Mets star pitcher. The agent also mentioned that Dwight was traveling to New York to check himself into the Scripps Clinic for drug addiction. I was advised that there was a **New York Daily News** reporter on board and told to see to it that Dwight was not to be disturbed or interviewed by this tenacious reporter. You know how the papparazzi can be. Two of my friends were traveling to New York as well... Larry and Judy Nero. I had them upgraded to first class on the B727 so that first class would be filled up to preclude this predator from disturbing Dwight. I had a lengthy conversation with Dwight pertaining to his career and the possibility of his induction into the Baseball Hall of

Fame, if he would only stay off the drugs and heed my warning. Apparently, my fatherly talk fell on deaf ears, based on his later life. Upon landing and taxiing to the gate, I kept a close eye out for the reporter. Sensing that the reporter would try to harass Dwight while deplaning I positioned myself in between the partition separating the first class cabin from the tourist cabin. I felt myself being pushed. It was the reporter, attempting to gain access to the first class cabin. I stepped back and proceeded to step on this reporter's foot. When the reporter threatened me with a lawsuit, I advised him that in the Delta Air Lines printed schedule, a Federal Air Regulation states that "Any person who interferes with an airline flight, be it on the ground or in the air, is subject to a fine or imprisonment" and told him to govern himself accordingly. The Port of New York Authority Police escorted Dwight off the aircraft, down the jet-way into an awaiting police car.

The next day and the succeeding two weeks turned out to be the saddest days for my entire family and for people all over the world. The wedding took place in Massapequa, Long Island, NY at 14:00 April 03, 1987 with a reception scheduled at 16:00 at the Sands catering facility in Lido Beach, NY. Subsequent to the ceremony, we decided to stop at the Long Island Marriott Hotel in Uniondale for a drink and then head to the reception. We then proceeded on the Meadowbrook Parkway crossed the bridge towards Jones Beach, made a right turn onto the Loop Parkway and proceeded on Lido Boulevard, a four-lane divided highway, to the Sands. When we arrived at the Sands catering establishment, there were police cars on the scene. It appeared there was an accident, involving two cars; one was a blue limousine and the other a black Pontiac Trans Am, a high performance car. The Nassau County Policeman stopped me, directed me to move on. When I told him that I was a member of the wedding party's family, he directed me to take a circuitous route to the parking lot. Determining that this was a secured crime scene due to auto deaths, I parked my car and approached the Sands; in doing so I had to side step two black zippered leather body bags. It suddenly dawned on me that this was not going to be a festive occasion. As we spoke, two ambulances arrived and transported the bride and maid of honor to Nassau Medical Center. I ascertained that the groom and best man, the Phillips brothers were dead... killed instantly at the hands of a maniac. I scanned the accident scene and learned that the limo was traveling westbound and had been broad sided while attempting to cross the eastbound lane of Lido Boulevard to enter the Sands facility. The limo had been virtually cut in half and wrapped around a concrete pole, some seventy-five feet from the point of impact. According to the police report and the next morning's newspapers, two autos were drag racing on the eastbound lane of Lido Boulevard, at a speed of one hundred miles an hour around a curve and impacted the limo in the vicinity of the rear right door. Debra, the maid of honor and the bride's sister, was thrown clear and survived, however, severely injured. The driver survived uninjured. The autos drag racing, were a Pontiac Trans AM muscle car and a Chevy Camaro. The Chevy missed the limo and was never identified, even to this day. The bride, Carol Anne Zagorski Phillips was married for an hour and a half before becoming a widow. She lived for twenty-one days before she passed away and joined her new husband in Heaven. It is quite sad that the quality of life, here on Earth, is diminished by occurrences similar to this.

The song that Eric Clapton composed for his departed son, entitled "Tears From Heaven" poignantly applies to these two unfortunate lovers. This is an example of God's gift of "Free Will," whereby He gives us the gift to pick and choose our destiny. One happy note... Debra, the maid of honor and Doug Krapata, the driver of my cousin Joe Zagorski's Limo Service were married two years later. This event was covered nationally and internationally for the duration of the life of the bride and the eventual trial and conviction of the driver. He received a sentence of two and one half to seven years for killing three people. For me, this was assault with a deadly weapon and a clear case of vehicular manslaughter.

Chapter Thirteen:

B757 / B767, State of the Art Training and Flying, October 03, 1987 to January 25, 1993

Delta Air Lines purchased Boeing 757s, and Boeing 767 200s for domestic travel, plus the Boeing 767ER (Extended Range) for international travel. The Boston domicile was scheduled to receive some of the flying in 1987. I was starting to become fairly senior on the B727 and as a result of attrition, my time on the B727 was coming to an end and I had nine years left to fly before I would attain the age of sixty, the mandatory retirement age at the time. The retirement age has since been increased to sixty-five because the philosophy has changed. However, the experience level has diminished as a result of early retirements triggered by multiple airline filings of Chapter Eleven, mergers and the fuel crisis.

I was a successful bidder on a B-757/767 in Boston, which entailed almost two months of intensive training. The training included the new "glass cockpit" concept. Instead of analog instruments, everything is CRTs or cathode ray tubes. Quite a few of the older pilots refused the upgrade training on the new concept. *"You cannot teach an old dog new tricks."* The most humiliating thing to any pilot is to "wash out" of a program. I made it through; but it was a bear and I was fifty-one years old. There was a saying in training alluding to the fact that the instructors presented this new curriculum to the students with the velocity of a "fire hose." It was force- fed to us by chief ground instructor, Charley Gersback. The training consisted of one separate rating on two different aircraft, the B757 and B767, which was double trouble. The B757 was a narrow-bodied aircraft and the B767 a wide-bodied aircraft. Initially, my flying was almost exclusively on the B757, which was like a "sports car" and great fun to fly. You had to plan ahead, especially on descent; otherwise they would have to shoot you down… it just wouldn't stop flying *"Just kidding."*

Delta acquired Western Airlines in 1987 and my buddy Dick Calarco, came onboard as a Delta captain with more seniority than I. This merger gave me the opportunity to fly throughout the northwest, including Salt Lake City, UT, Portland, OR and Seattle, WA. It was a pleasant change of scenery. One of the perks associated with a merger is that you get to fly with people from a different part of the country with different philosophies. This was the case with the Delta/Western merger. I had been offered a pilot position with Western in 1962 and turned it down due to the drastic move to the west coast. My buddy, Dick Calarco moved out there in 1961 and was well acclimated to the Northwest Territory. One of the subjects associated with the merger that Dick and I discussed was "female pilots" as they were fairly new on the scene at that time. Dick said that Western had a female first officer who was absolutely drop dead gorgeous. Her name was Valerie Walker Patton. She was five foot nine inches tall, slender and absolutely the most beautiful woman alive with long straight blond hair, which fell below her shoulder blades. Dick said that when he flew with her on the B727, he could not help but become distracted by her beauty and the aroma of her provocative expensive perfume wafting throughout the confines of the miniscule cockpit. During my appointed rounds throughout the Northwest Territory, I happened to gaze upon this Gorgeous Goddess on a few occasions and I too was quite smitten by her beauty. It turns out her father was Clint Walker, the actor who portrayed Posey in the movie "The Dirty Dozen" and Cheyenne Bodie on a western TV series. Valerie was quite a capable pilot and a joy to look at as opposed to an overweight male first officer, don't you agree?

I was at the Hilton in Portland, OR on an overnight; the hotel was swarming with all kinds of security, both local and federal. I did some investigating and discovered that the US Navy ship, Vincennes, was docked near the hotel and Captain William Rogers was staying at the Hilton. The Vincennes shot down an Iran Air A300 Airbus on July 03, 1988.

On August 31, 1989, I had just checked into the same Hilton at 11:30 PDST (Pacific Daylight Savings Time) and the front desk had a message for me to contact my oldest daughter on Long Island.

I spoke with my daughter and she told me that my father had passed away that morning in Patchogue, NY. I made arrangements to fly the aircraft the next morning to Salt Lake and then deadhead, (ride as a passenger) to New York to attend the funeral.

The date was September 05, 1989 and I had an overnight in Palm Beach, FL while domiciled in Boston. We were provided accommodations at the Marriott Hotel at the intersection of PGA Boulevard and I-95, some eight miles north of the Palm Beach International Airport. Upon rising, I decided to have breakfast at the hotel and read the local newspaper, which was The Palm Beach Post. While scanning through the newspaper, I noticed an advertisement for a new condominium development with the name of Island Dunes on South Hutchinson Island. South Hutchinson Island is thirty-five miles north of the Palm Beach Airport and would be an ideal place for a second winter home. I contacted the real estate office and was advised that there were two buildings being built and that there were condos available in building two at pre-construction prices. I decided that on my next days off I would head south and check out the area and the condo scene. This venture would be ideal in that I could get away from the cold dismal climate of New York in winter and *"chill out."* I purchased a condo on the eighth floor, overlooking the ocean and the pool area. I took possession on October 31, 1989. The condo enabled me to get away for about four days between trips and gave me the opportunity to study for my annual proficiency check and recurrent training in a pleasant atmosphere without any distractions. During one of these breaks, I decided to take my books and study by the pool. It was ten o'clock in the morning and the pool was quite deserted. While totally engrossed in the FMC (Flight Management Computer) section of my flight manual, the sprinkler system at the pool activated and sprayed water all over the occupants and their belongings. I jumped up and dashed for the condominium office on the first floor of my building to report the malfunction. I spoke to Ginny, the manager's secretary and she made a telephone call and corrected the problem. I thanked her and went back to studying for my PC (Proficiency Check). I was totally engrossed in my studying once again when a pretty lady approached me and thanked me for getting the sprinkler systems errant timer corrected. Her name was Pamela Lavino from the Philadelphia Main Line, from a town called Blue Bell, which I never heard of. Her husband's name was Ted and was from the Lavino Shipping Family of Philadelphia. I understand there is a Lavino Hall at Villanova University donated by the Lavino Family. Pam asked about myself, I told her that I worked for the airlines and that I was studying when the sprinklers went off. She said that her brother, George worked for Delta Air Lines and was domiciled in Boston. Small world. I told her that I, too, worked for Delta out of Boston and asked her brother's name. She said George Fogwell. Coincidentally, I was one of the first captains that George flew with when he was a flight engineer on the B727 out of Boston. I became quite friendly with Pam and Ted and with another couple, named Arthur and Lee Falk from Atlantic City, NJ. Arthur was a gynecologist originally from Bensonhurst, Brooklyn, and passed away December 03, 2007. He is greatly missed. I equated him to a Jewish Santa Claus. Arthur was a genius.

As I stated in one of the opening chapters of this autobiography, I was fascinated with radio waves, especially short wave transmissions. While living at the condo, I purchased a short wave radio from Radio Shack along with a short wave antenna, consisting of a roll of 120' of multi-stranded copper wire. I wound it around the aluminum railing or suspended the antenna in the trees or shrubs on the shore. I listened to Gander Radio in Newfoundland or Shanwick Radio in Europe, which relays aircraft possession reports to air traffic control facilities for the airliners crossing the pond (Atlantic Ocean). It was a busman's holiday for me as I am an inquisitive kid at heart, even to this day. I still listen to Miami Radio, which is in contact with aircraft proceeding to and from South America. While surfing the short wave radio bands at the condo, I discovered a broadcast that was in a language fairly familiar to me: Latin, which I studied in preparation to becoming an altar boy for the Catholic Church. I realized that it was the Prayers of the Rosary, the Our Father and the Hail Mary. The program commenced at 14:40 to 15:00 EST (Eastern Standard Time) every day of the week. Upon doing some research, I discovered that it was Vatican Radio from Rome, Italy. In the world of modern day computers, it is now broadcast on the Internet in what is called streaming radio; therefore, I listen to it on my computer through Real Player or Windows Media Player applications.

Piccolo Mondo *(small world)*

I had just completed a trip and had five days off; I spent them at my condo in Jensen Beach, FL. I decided to visit a restaurant and bar named, "Mr. Laffs," situated on the Indian River. Sunday afternoon was a great time to dine with friends and listen to great music. We ordered some munchies and I consumed a bucket of rocks, which is six miniature bottles of Rolling Rock beer brewed in Latrobe, PA. During the consumption process, a 42' fire engine red cigarette race boat docked at the marina with two gentlemen and a drop-dead gorgeous young blonde in a gold bikini. I had a problem focusing on the company at hand without staring at the blond. About fifteen minutes after the grand arrival, one gentleman and his beautiful bikini clad girlfriend approached my table and presented me with a Rolling Rock ball cap. He said, "We Rolling Rock people had to stick together." I thanked him and exited the scene an hour later. In four days, I returned to New York and flew my next trip out of Boston. On a Sunday afternoon some two weeks later, I decided to go to a restaurant at Westhampton's Gabreski Airport in NY. With my Rolling Rock ball cap on to protect me from the summer sun, plus being the creature of habit I am (aren't we all?) I ordered a Rolling Rock and became involved in a conversation with the bartender pertaining to the incident at Mr. Laff's in Jensen Beach. The bartender stated that it had to be John Morgan, the east coast sales representative for Rolling Rock. No sooner than the words emanated from his mouth, did the gentleman from Rolling Rock appear on the scene. He recognized my hat and me and we struck up a conversation. He introduced himself as the illustrious John Morgan. I asked him if this was his primary job or was there something else he did for a living? John told me he was a teacher and a sports director for the Middle Island School District at Longwood High School. I said that my two daughters went to Longwood. When he learned my name was Nick Gravino, he revealed that he had actually coached my daughter Leslie, in softball. I exclaimed, "Get out of here, you have to be kidding!" In conclusion… "It's a Small World After All," to quote Disney once again.

As time progressed, Delta Air Lines received different models of aircraft, and we had to read up on the differences; however, they all flew the same.

There was a B757/B767 first officer named Robert Buck (Robbie Buck) whose father was a TWA (Trans World Airlines) captain and a famous author. Rob's father wrote a book entitled "North Star Over My Shoulder." Robbie and I flew a trip from Boston to Atlanta and on to

Bermuda and return. It was a great trip and we truly enjoyed flying together, especially the Atlanta to Bermuda portion. As we approached Bermuda from the northwest, we noticed that there was a cloud deck at two thousand feet and that we would be landing to the northwest, which meant that we had to circle the island from the south. We requested an altitude of one thousand five hundred feet so that we would be below the cloud deck and give our paying passengers a grand tour of this beautiful island. It was quite impressive with all the stark white concrete tile roofs and Bermuda pink exteriors. They use white concrete tile roofs because Bermudians recycle the rainwater to compensate for the scarcity of water on the island... just a little tad of trivia. As we flew under the cloud deck, Robbie pointed out all the areas of interest on this tropical paradise. After our landing, our passengers could not thank us enough for the grand tour.

In 1991, Delta Air Lines acquired a portion of Pan American Airways for their International Routes out of JFK in New York. To fly those routes, initially, Delta acquired a substandard aircraft, in my estimation, known as the Airbus A310. Any aircraft manufacturer that has to utilize the vertical fin in the tail to store fuel is not doing something right. Reluctantly, I bid the A310 out of New York to fly internationally because the end of my career was near. I received my final rating in the A310 on May 11, 1992, which was the last rating of my career. I was not impressed with the aircraft after flying the far superior B767ER. The thing that blew my mind, which did not instill confidence in this foreign aircraft, was the first video on the first day of Airbus A310 ground school. It consisted of an A310 test pilot narrating a fully automated coupled approach (autopilot approach) with a coupled missed approach, which was accomplished without the assistance of the flight crew whatsoever. It took place at the Airbus factory in Toulouse, France. The approach takes place at ten miles from the airport of intended landing while the test pilot is narrating the approach and what was to be a fully automated missed approach to minimums or about one hundred feet above ground. I watched this movie from a ground-based camera, narrated by a test pilot who was also on the ground. The test pilot explained what was going on in the cockpit and what was going to transpire during the fully automated missed approach. As he continued the narration below the trees, there was a big cloud of smoke raging skyward where the aircraft should have executed the missed approach. It now became a crash site. The accident investigation concluded that there was a glitch within the onboard computers. Instead of going around, the aircraft crashed on the runway and did not respond to the pilot's input at the controls. They were unable to disconnect the autopilot and execute the missed approach manually.

I recall another incident, whereby, a Northwest Airlines Airbus A320 was in a holding pattern on autopilot and the on-board computers would not permit the aircraft to leave the holding pattern, regardless of what the crew did to correct the situation. After this demonstration, I developed some doubts pertaining to the reliability of this foreign aircraft constructed by the French. As I said earlier, *"**Boeing builds them better.**"* I received the rating and three bounces (three landings and takeoffs). All I needed was the international ground school and I would have been good to go. Luckily, I was cancelled and returned to Boston on my dearest B-757/767 aircraft. I flew domestically out of Boston until January 25, 1993.

"What was that Mysterious Green Arrow"?

This has all the makings of a comic book mystery classic. On one particular trip out of Boston, I was advised that we were to ferry (fly empty for ship distribution) a brand spanking new B767 ER (extended range) aircraft from Atlanta to Orlando. We had the differences fact sheets on the aircraft; therefore, everything was legal. We were en route to Orlando and were, *"flying along in flight,"* when I noticed that there was a green arrow going round and round on the ADF instrument (automatic direction finding), totally out of control. This was used during low frequency ADF approaches and/or airways. I checked on the differences sheets, but they did not address the green arrow. It was very disconcerting, especially since we were unable to extinguish the green arrow. Upon arrival, I asked the next crew how to put out the arrow and nobody seemed to know. It was quite some time before I discovered that the green arrow was searching for a valid low frequency radio station to point to. If the LF radio did not have a valid signal, it would search. There were two options: 1. Tune in a valid LF radio station or, 2. Turn it off. So ends the saga of the *Mysterious Green Arrow*.

Chapter Fourteen:

International Flying, the End is Near, January 26, 1993 to May 16, 1996

O n January 26, 1993, after attending international ground school, I was assigned with international line check Captain Ron Stowe to deadhead from Atlanta to Cincinnati, depart Cincinnati International Airport, destination New Delhi, India via Frankfurt, Germany and return. It consisted of an overnight in Frankfurt then on to New Delhi, overnight and another overnight in Frankfurt and then on back to Cincinnati, finally deadheading to Atlanta... a total of nine days. This trip was quite demanding. We had to fly around Iraq and Iran and over the Himalayas via Afghanistan, which required added oxygen for passengers and crew because the minimum safe altitude is above 18,000 feet mean sea level in that area due to high mountainous terrain.

There were further problems: communicating with some of these third-world foreign countries, namely Kabul, Afghanistan. The procedures call for contacting the next country on your route of flight ten minutes prior to entering the boundary and if there is no contact, you were not to proceed any further, for fear of being shot down. These third-world countries are members of ICAO (International Civil Aviation Organization) where English is the accepted universal language. However, they do not always comprehend what they are saying. As a result, there have been a few aircraft disasters. One was an Avianca DC8 that ran out of fuel and crashed on tennis star, John MacEnroe's father's estate on the North Shore of Long Island. The crew did not know when to say, **"MAY DAY," the international distress call.** Back to my story, they were still operating with substandard radio navigation and communications equipment from the 1940s, which consisted of vacuum tube radios and low frequency radio navigational aids.

We landed at three in the morning, India time, and were escorted by an elderly armed guard who sported a gigantic handlebar moustache and a single shot eight-gauge shotgun. He looked like a Gurka. The mode of transportation for the pilots only, (the flight attendants were domiciled in New Delhi), was a motorcycle with a cart attached that carried four people. It resembled a motorized rickshaw. It was known as a "Tuk, tuk", which came from the sound of its two-cycle lawn mower engine exhaust. I equate the ride to the Delhi Hilton as a "demolition derby," or survival of the fittest. The traffic lights were turned off at that hour of the morning and we were on our own. They should have provided us with gas masks for the fumes from the "Tuk tuk." The male crewmembers arranged to meet for breakfast and tour the city, which was an experience in itself. I was quite concerned with the pollutants in the water and the lack of cleanliness. For that reason, I took a shower with a shower cap over my eyes, nose and ears to ward off any infection. We met downstairs and proceeded to the restaurant for breakfast. I ordered Corn Flakes and milk, figuring it was something simple. As I devoured the Corn Flakes, I detected a problem: one of the Corn Flakes almost broke my tooth. On close examination, I discovered it was a hardened kernel of corn. Subsequent to that horrendous trip, the only Delhi I want to visit is the Stage Deli in Manhattan. The trip back to the *Good Old U.S. of A,* uneventful and the check pilot released me to fly internationally on my own.

In February of 1993, I was awarded a schedule that consisted of four trips to Moscow. February is not an ideal month to visit Moscow. In preparation for the trip, I went to SEARS and purchased thermal underwear, a ski jacket, ski mittens, ski cap, and thermal shoepacks. It was quite an interesting trip, in that Russian altimetry is very different from that in the free world.

> Russian air traffic control uses meters instead of feet for assigned altitudes; everyone else uses feet according to ICAO (International Civil Aviation Organization). Therefore, one person in the cockpit had to use a published table to convert, so that we could supply the flight management system with the corresponding feet equating to the required meters. Another problem with Russian airspace: the pictorial display of the FMS (Flight Management System) jumped from time to time, because the Russians provided the free world with erroneous latitude and longitude coordinates for navigational fixes within Russia, in case of war. Incidentally, Russian Airliners are constructed with a bombardier's compartment in the nose of the aircraft. I would assume the aircraft is also fitted with a set of full-functioning bomb-bay doors. Upon arriving at the gate at Sheremetyevo Airport in Moscow, a Russian soldier boarded first and collected the crew's passports. It took the crew at least forty-five minutes to clear customs and immigration, a clear case of Russian harassment. Russia also requires that you declare all the gold and diamonds on your person. Money is a problem, too. You are not permitted to take Russian rubles out of the country and you must declare how much money you have and the denomination of the bills. What a crock.

The ride to the hotel was in overcrowded substandard vans with substandard heaters. The hotel, on the other hand, was a five-star hotel, owned by Lufthansa Airlines near the Olympic Stadium...quite adequate. Moscow is rather dismal with prevalent poverty, including bread lines. The streetlights consisted of strings of incandescent light bulbs a la an

Italian Festival. Taxi service was provided by anyone with a vehicle. I got to visit Red Square, Lenin's Tomb, the Kremlin and the Gum, a department store across Red Square and Saint Basil's, a famous church at the end of Red Square. We went out to dinner at a restaurant called, "Tren Mos," which stands for Trenton, NJ and Moscow. Two brothers owned it, and as you probably guessed, one was from Trenton, NJ and the other from Moscow. Incidentally, the Russian Mafia eventually killed the brother from Moscow. I also went to a Japanese Steak House off Red Square. I paid $60.00 in U.S. money for a measly piece of substandard steak, miniature shrimp and a handful of veggies. This would have cost about $25.00 in the States.

Upon departure the next morning, there was a five-star brunch, consisting of European and American delicacies, buffet style. We were serenaded by two absolutely gorgeous female harpists in traditional Russian costumes. All in all, my stay in Moscow was quite educational.

On one of my return trips from Moscow to JFK, passengers were still permitted to smoke on the aircraft. This was especially devastating for me; I suffer from acute sinusitis attacks. I received notification from a flight attendant that there were two passengers, a husband and wife in business class who were bothered by the smoke, so they requested to be upgraded to first class. This class upgrade was forbidden in flight, it had to be arranged on the ground prior to departure, due to customs declarations and security. The flight attendant advised them that this was not possible. The passengers persisted to distract the flight attendants, up to a point that they were unable to tend to their required duties. I, in turn, sent the relief pilot to speak to the husband. Incidentally, according to the FAA, on any flight of more than eight hours and less than twelve hours, a relief pilot is required to break up the monotony and provide some quiet time away from the cockpit. For the pilots, Delta provided the flight crews with an extra jump seat in the cockpit. Other airlines provide their flight crews with a rest seat in first class. The rest accommodations were absolutely horrible and barbaric. The FAA also requires that any flight in excess of twelve hours or more be equipped with two complete flight crews.

The relief pilot returned from talking to the husband and reported that he and his wife claimed they had been promised first class seats if the smoking bothered them. I relayed this message to the company and the company replied in the negative. I had the flight attendant explain to the passengers that we contacted the company and according to regulations, they had to stay in business class for the remainder of the flight. I, then, received a request from the flight attendant that these passengers wanted to see a copy of our Federal Air Regulations (FARs). I stated that we are not permitted to have our manuals leave the cockpit during a flight; however, we would be glad to have these passengers view our FARs subsequent to the flight. After about an hour, the flight attendant said these passengers were now asking for the regulations pertaining to smoking sections. They were informed that information is enclosed in their ticket packets provided by the ticket counter or reservations. Next, these passengers requested to see the captain. I sent word that I was unable to talk with them at this time due to flight duties and that I would come back and speak with them. I finally took my break and advised the flight attendant to have this irate passenger come to the cockpit door to discuss his problems. This man approached me and presented me his card; he was an attorney from the Colorado Springs area. He demanded that he be upgraded for the remainder of the flight, which was about another five hours to JFK. He stated that he would pursue legal action if his requests were not fulfilled. I told him that this was impossible and that it would be settled on the ground. He began to rant and rave and was starting to become a pain in the butt. I warned him that he was interfering with a flight and advised that Federal Air Regulations state that, "Anyone who interferes with a flight, either on the ground or in the air, will be subject to a fine or imprisonment." Therefore, I suggested that he govern himself accordingly. With that, I terminated the discussion because I had to be present in the cockpit when our domestic clearance was received from Gander center.

We were en route from Gander to New York when we received a call from the flight attendant that the passengers were acting up once more and required that we turn on the *"no smoking"* sign. With that, I told the flight attendant that I would have the proper authorities meet the aircraft, namely the Port of New York Authority police and the Delta station manager. Consequently, upon landing and arrival at the gate, there was a Port Authority police car waiting. When the forward cabin door was opened, there were two Port Authority policemen and the Delta station manager waiting. I introduced the officials to the passengers and they were escorted off the aircraft. I cleared customs and immigration and proceeded to return home to Port Jefferson, NY. The following Monday, I contacted the Delta station manager and inquired as to the problems and solution to this incident. It seems that this couple had traveled to Moscow a week earlier via economy class and Delta misplaced the husband's luggage. After two days and no luggage, Delta agreed to reimburse this passenger for clothing, toilet articles, etc. and upgrade the couple to business class on the return trip. The couple requested first class on the way home and Delta declined, stating that only one level upgrade is required. Delta finally found the man's baggage four days into their stay in Moscow. Apparently, the lost luggage was the root of the problem we encountered on the way home. In this case, the passenger was in the wrong. Passengers can be known to make flights quite difficult for the flight crews.

My international flights were a great joy for me. My career was coming to an end. On June 05, 1994, I was the captain of Delta Flight 148 from JFK to FCO (Rome Fumicino). We departed at 17:30 and were scheduled to be in Rome at 09:30. On June 06, 1994 at exactly 05:30 GMT (Greenwich Mean Time), our position was exactly over the Normandy Beachhead in France at exactly sunrise, fifty years after the Invasion of France at Normandy by the Allied Armed Forces. I have the only picture in existence, with the time and the date, of that auspicious occasion (included in the Exhibit section). There was a cloud cover over the entire area and we were at 35,000 feet, which was above the clouds; therefore, no one on the ground saw the **Sunrise over Normandy.**

It was October 31, 1994, unbeknownst to my crew and me, we had the great distinction of flying the first Delta Air Lines B767-ER to Ben Gurion International Airport in Tel Aviv. This flight had been formerly accomplished with the Airbus A310 from Pan American. Being the tightest secured airport in the world, we were quite shocked when we were greeted with a band and all kinds of dignitaries and festivities. The crew was presented with plaques, SABRA,(Israeli liquor), and an invitation to dinner at the hotel where we spent the night. Unfortunately, we had to decline the dinner because we were scheduled for the early morning flight back to Frankfurt, Germany.

We should tailor our airport security procedures to those of the Israelis. I had been made aware of El Al's (Israel's national airline) stringent procedures at JFK when I was an agent for Northeast Airlines in the 1950s. Their procedures go something like this: There are two Port Authority police cars alongside the runway when El Al touches down. The police cars escort the aircraft to an isolated pad on the Tarmac, a holding area quite a distance from the main terminal. No jet-ways, consequently, no bomb threats. The aircraft is cordoned off with stanchions and security put in place at strategic points around the aircraft. The passengers are put onto specially constructed busses that house a jackscrew mechanism. The bus can move up and down to accommodate various terminal levels. The luggage is transported to a baggage claim area where the passenger clears. El Al's philosophy is that the luggage stays with the passenger. If the passenger is boarded on the aircraft, the luggage is boarded. If the passenger is denied boarding, the luggage is removed. All luggage has to be accounted for on all departures and arrivals, no exceptions. These procedures are standard wherever El Al flies. I admire Israel; it is a no nonsense country. We need more of their procedures in our country. We don't have the chutzpah.

Now to digress a little, during my many years of flying, I can honestly say that I have never encountered any problems pertaining to drugs or alcohol on the job. Initially, the rule was *"**No alcohol for twenty-four hours**"* from bottle to throttle; however, in the 90s it was changed to eight hours. There were all kinds of checks and balances to preclude any problems from occurring. To illustrate, I had an incident in Boston. It was a rainy evening and the inbound aircraft was delayed due to inclement weather and air traffic control. The crew was assembled at the departure gate area and a distinguished executive-type gentleman approached us and complained about the lengthy delay. I immediately detected alcohol on his breath. He said that he had been in the passenger lounge awaiting the aircraft. I stated that I detected the smell of alcohol on his breath and I asked that he kindly remove himself from our presence and address his concerns with the agent behind the desk. This was to guard against other passengers coming to the erroneous conclusion (from smelling alcohol nearby) that their crew had been drinking and that we would be removed from flight status. In the eyes of the FAA and the airline, we as a crew are guilty until proven innocent. Any incident would have created a lengthy delay. The airline would have had to replace the crewmembers.

Many years ago, there was a B727 crew (which I was not part of) consisting of pilots and flight attendants. The flight was from Tampa to Detroit. Upon arrival in Detroit, the pilots went and had their shoes shined at a local stand in the terminal. On the return trip, a flight attendant came up to the cockpit and detected the smell of the shoe polish and erroneously decided that the pilots were drinking. Upon arrival at their domicile, the male pilots were met by a representative of the chief pilot's office and relieved from duty on the assumption that the shoe polish was alcohol.

There was another incident in the 1970s in which the airport was fogged in and the tower was closed. The crew decided to taxi up and down the runway, in an attempt to dissipate the fog so that the flight would be able to take off. This was exposed in the newspapers and the pilots were reprimanded.

In a similar scenario, a fog condition existed at an airport early one morning. The tower instructed the flight to taxi down the runway and take off in the opposite direction because the wind was calm and the RVR (Runway Visual Range) that governs landings and takeoffs was above minimums for the takeoff portion of the flight. A flight attendant on board, aware of the previous related incident, erroneously reported this incident to the flight attendant supervisor who in turn, reported it to the chief pilot's office. The pilots were brought on the carpet to explain their actions. Of course, the charges were dropped because the FAA controller in the Tower initiated it.

In the latter part of my career, while flying internationally, drug testing came into existence. Upon entering American airspace, our flight received a message from Atlanta flight operations that *"doctor pea body"* would greet the flight upon arrival at JFK and that crewmember *so and so* would be escorted through customs and immigration to a secure area, in which a sample of his or her urine would be taken. The procedure was similar to taking blood, except that the specimen's temperature was taken to verify its authenticity. Everything was labeled, and the donor signed a statement to the effect that it was a true and correct sample and acknowledged that there was no tampering with the specimen. Contrary to public opinion, flight personnel, especially older, mature pilots, are very conscientious individuals. I was accused one time for drinking a gin and tonic in the cockpit; not so, it was a club soda with a lime. Some people's minds run rampant. Enough said.

A Pilot's Memoirs

I came up with an analogy that most problems on aircraft are largely caused by individuals, especially the executive types, who develop a form of claustrophobia and paranoia. I believe that paranoia sets in upon entering an aluminum capsule because they have no control over the outcome of their destiny and they have to be in control at all times. They create problems and lash out at the crew. My philosophy has always been, "All seats on the aircraft get there at the same time, except mine gets there first." I have never worried about my passengers relative to who or what was on board etc. I was a true professional and never mixed business with pleasure. I totally concentrated on my flying and the comfort and safety of those who were put in my charge.

A medical emergency just came to mind. In 1995, I was doing a trip from JFK to Frankfurt, Germany. We were about two hours from landing and approaching the Irish coast in the vicinity of Shannon when I received a call from a flight attendant that a female passenger was having problem breathing and was showing symptoms of a heart attack. At that time, we carried a medical kit in the cockpit; there were no defibrillators available back then. She advised there was a doctor on board who required the use of the medical kit, which she secured without delay. I asked her to keep me posted. I had the relief pilot contact the company and advise them that we might have to land in Shannon, depending upon the doctor's diagnosis. The doctor told the attendant that it was definitely a heart attack and he needed to speak to me. When I spoke to him, the doctor said that the patient was resting comfortably, that he had done everything possible for her. However, he cautioned that if something else would occur between now and our arrival in Frankfurt, which was an hour and one half away, there would be nothing else he could do. Armed with that information, I elected to land at Shannon, Ireland. We contacted Shannon Air Traffic Control and Delta Airlines, stated we were diverting to Shannon and asked that they have the paramedics standing by to transport the woman to the nearest hospital. It took about twelve minutes to descend and land in Shannon. Actually, we arrived at the gate before the paramedics. It was 08:00 local time and they removed the woman from the aircraft and we proceeded on to Frankfurt. They could never criticize me for my decision to divert, because I valued human life above all. Better safe than sorry. This is why pilots should be allowed to fly after sixty years of age, providing they can meet the medical standards. The name of the game is "experience, experience, experience" and that comes with age, like vintage wine. The older it gets, the better it gets.

Many of my international flights into Kennedy airport consisted of a Canarsie approach landing on runway 13R or 13L. These approaches, which were called "Kamikaze" approaches originated from the southwest at Rockaway Point in Brooklyn, the gateway to New York Harbor. It entailed flying a VOR radial, (Visual Omni Range) overhead the Canarsie VOR, then flying the 041 radial outbound to pick up the high intensity strobe lead in lights on the ground, which were located alongside the Belt Parkway. These lights would split. One set took you overhead the old International Hotel (which had a series of lights on the roof) and would take you to runway 13R. The other took you to runway 13L, which had the three old hangars alongside the approach end of the runway. I worked there on the ground in the late 1950s in crew scheduling and flight dispatch. This is where the local knowledge came into play once more. I shot this approach, making sure I always stayed on the right side of the Belt Parkway and on the required radial. I passed the baseball fields at Lefferts Boulevard and paralleled the parkway until I could see the 130th street overpass and P.S. 124 grade school and kept the Belt Park Rest off my left, which was a bar on the corner of 130th Street and 135th Avenue, just off the Belt Parkway. I then executed a turn to the runway heading, picked up the International Hotel and the lead-in light on the roof if I was landing on the right side or picked up the three hangars if I was landing on the left side and stayed to the right of the hangars on final approach. These runways also had a VASI lighting system, (Visual Approach Slope Indicator), consisting of a combination of both red and white lights. The normal glide slope is three degrees and if you were on the proper rate of descent for the runway, the forward set of lights would be red and the rearward set of lights would be white. If you were too high, all the lights would be white and conversely, if you were too low, all the lights would be red. This is another example where my living at the gateway to Kennedy Airport and local knowledge and situation awareness saved the day. I used these procedures, in conjunction with the published approved approach procedures by the FAA, which governed the approach.

Besides Moscow and New Delhi, my international flying consisted of trips to Paris, Nice, Rome, Milan, Athens, Frankfurt, Hamburg, Amsterdam, Oslo, Denmark and Shannon. I would love have visited other European cities; however, I had to hang up my spurs and move on.

On June 24, 1995, I was in Rome preparing for the return trip to JFK on flight 149. The aircraft was situated on a "pad" on the tarmac and we were in the final boarding stages of our flight to New York. I was in my seat in the cockpit and I observed a white Delta van pull up to the jet way. Two men exited the van. They were clothed in black with little white collars, signifying they were clergy. It was quite obvious that they were Catholic priests, especially since Rome is the headquarters of the Catholic Church. I recognized the older priest as John Cardinal O'Connor from the Archdiocese of New York. I had known of Cardinal O'Connor for quite some time, being a practicing Catholic in New York. I had attended a Mass at St. Patrick's Cathedral in Manhattan for the souls of Pan American Flight 103 that was blown out of the sky over Lockerbie, Scotland by Muslim Terrorists. I immediately left my seat and proceeded down the high ramp to greet him. It is a Catholic tradition to kiss a Cardinal's ring, since the Pope blessed it. As I reached for his hand, the Cardinal tripped and I caught him. I introduced myself and he introduced me to his associate and personal assistant. I then introduced the Cardinal to the flight attendants and escorted him to his seat in first class. Prior to the departure, we were advised by Rome air traffic control that there would be an hour and one half delay due to congestion on the Atlantic routes across the Atlantic Ocean. I advised the Cardinal of the delay and explained I would try to have the delay rescinded. I had the relief pilot contact Atlanta flight control to try and have the delay rescinded because we had Cardinal O'Connor on board. Atlanta flight control responded with a message from dispatcher Gil Chapman, "I don't even think the Pope could change the European ATC problems." With that, I instructed the relief pilot to contact Fumicino (Rome) air traffic control clearance delivery and tell them that we had Cardinal O'Connor on board and had just come from an urgent meeting with Pope John Paul II and had to hurry back to New York. It was quite apparent that this little *"white lie"* did the trick. We left on time and arrived ahead of schedule.

I became quite friendly with the Cardinal throughout the remaining years of his life. He was a great man. He was a Chaplin at the United States Naval Academy at Annapolis, MD for a long time. My wife and I would attend Mass at St. Patrick's Cathedral and when Pope John Paul II came to America on October 04, 1995, the thirtieth anniversary of my flying career with the airlines, we received tickets to attend Mass at Aqueduct Race Track, adjacent to the high school I attended some forty years earlier. Cardinal O'Connor passed away on May 03, 2000 and I attended his funeral at St. Pat's. I was seated in the second row behind Kofi Anon of United Nations fame. It was a sad day; the Catholic Church lost a great leader and I lost a great friend.

In July of 1995, I developed a severe case of acute sinusitis, due to the smoking on the international flights. I wound up with a middle ear infection that affected my equilibrium. The end result was that I had to have surgery on my nose and was off schedule for a month and a half.

My career was hanging in the balance and I sought the help of my good friend and retired chief pilot, Pete Loranger. He put me in contact with some specialists. I had the operation and completed my career. I went back to Boston and flew domestically for a couple of months until Delta abolished smoking on all its international flights. Domestic flights had been non-smoking flights for quite some time. When the no-smoking ban went into effect on international flights, I transferred back to international flying out of New York and finished my career on May 19, 1996.

In October of 1995, I was flying a sequence that consisted of a round trip from Boston to Reagan National Airport in Washington, DC. It was a night trip and as usual, we had to execute a visual river approach (Kamikaze) from the northwest down the Potomac, landing to the south in DC. The requirement was to maintain visual contact with the river, so as not to disturb the congressmen and to avoid the restricted areas associated with the White House. This approach is time consuming and quite demanding. There are many altitude restrictions and a series of twists and turns to get to runway 18. You are only on the final approach to Runway 18 for a few seconds prior to touchdown. It is for this reason that every departure and arrival is an air show and there are so many hard landings in DC. The runway is short and there is water on the south side. This is the only airport owned and operated by the FAA. *"Don't do as I do, do as I say."* The requirements for departure back then were as follows: if you were departing to the north, upon crossing the departure end of the runway boundary, you had to turn to a northwesterly heading and visually follow the river plus reduce power to bare minimum. This created an abnormal angle of attack at a critical time with not much altitude below you as a cushion in case of an engine failure, which normally would occur during high power settings as on take-off. There is an old saying that in a situation like this, you would be, *"hanging on the prop,"* or close to a stall. A stall in an aircraft is when there is a loss of lift due to an excessive angle of attack or an excessive angle of bank. A good Website to go to for a more technical definition is http://en.wikipedia.org/wiki/Stall_(flight).

On this particular evening, my first officer was flying the approach in the vicinity of the Watergate complex, made famous by the Nixon era, and we were *"cruising down the river"* at 1500 feet above the ground and some five miles from touchdown. We suddenly hit two huge birds; one struck just above the cockpit windows and the other inboard of the right engine. It was quite a jolt. The first officer asked what we should do. I checked all the engine parameters. Everything was normal. Rather than go around and exacerbate the situation and reenter this Kamikaze approach, I said, "Let's land this sucker." Upon inspection, we determined that there was no damage, entered it into the logbook and departed on time for Boston.

I had another bird experience while departing Atlanta for West Palm Beach. We were departing runway 09L in Atlanta and came in contact with a *"Pair of Phenalia's or a Pack of Derms"* (*just kidding.*), there were two gulls flying in formation at about 1500 feet. The birds were ingested into the left engine and instantly the cockpit filled with the aroma of rotisserie-roasted bird, a la Boston Market. Here again, I surveyed the engine parameters and various other systems for anomalies. There were none so we proceeded on to West Palm Beach. Upon arrival, the mechanic and I examined the engine. There was no damage; however, the smell of roast chicken prevailed while the right engine had an aroma of kerosene vintage 1995.

I returned to international flying in October of 1995 and flew out of JFK until my retirement. The remainder of my career was quite pleasant. I concentrated my flying by bidding Rome, Milan, Nice and Athens. I recall being assigned a sequence that consisted of a trip from JFK to Athens, Greece. Upon completion of my extensive paper work, route planning, map drawing, loading the flight plan into the FMS (Flight Management System) etc., I was proceeding to get settled for the ten-hour trip to Athens. A well-manicured and well-dressed young man appeared in my cockpit and presented his credentials. He was part of the Delta station manager's staff at JFK. The young man stated that today on board was a Saudi Arabian prince with an entourage of thirty-two people, who purchased all of first class. The remainder of the people was in business class. This young man requested that I permit the prince to smoke during the crossing, since the previous captain permitted it on the westbound crossing. I stated that it was against company policy and it would create problems and not be fair to the other passengers. Therefore, I would not permit it. I also stated that I would have to call in sick and delay the flight until a new captain arrived because of my acute sinusitis condition. Needless to say, the prince did not smoke on my flight.

While in Athens and staying at the Intercontinental Hotel, I was waiting in the lobby around six o'clock in the evening to go to the Plaka for dinner when who walks by but Yanni and Linda Evans, on their way to Yanni's world famous concert at the Acropolis. The ticket scalpers wanted $385 in U.S. currency for one ticket.

I was quite busy setting up my pension and numerous tasks associated with retirement. I was commuting between my condominium in Jensen Beach, FL and my home in Port Jefferson, NY. We had the Port Jefferson home up for sale so that we would move lock, stock and barrel to Florida and live happily ever after upon my retirement. I was in quite a quandary about where I wanted my career to terminate. It was a toss up between Rome and Milan. Due to schedules and monetary reasons, I chose Milan. The schedule consisted of two trips back to back to Milan, May 14th, 15th and 16th and then May 17th, May 18th and May 19th. I had sold my home on Long Island one month before retirement and was living in Jensen Beach, FL. I therefore spent the night of the 16th at a hotel on Long Island. The Catholic Feast of the Ascension of Jesus Christ, a holy day of obligation, just happened to be that night; therefore,

I attended Mass with my wife who came up to be on my last flight. St. Agnes Cathedral in Rockville Center, Long Island is the cathedral for the Diocese of Rockville Center. One of the rituals during Mass is to say, "Peace be with you" to the people around you. I, therefore, bestowed this blessing to the individuals within close proximity. As I turned to the people behind me, I noticed the tall good-looking actor, Adam West of Batman fame, whom I understand had a home in Oceanside, Long Island. Without thinking, I shook his hand and uttered the words, "Peace be with you, Batman." He in turn said to me, "And also with you" with a gigantic smile on his face. I guess I made his day as he made mine.

Chapter Fifteen:

My Last Flight, The Last Hurrah
May 17, 1996 to May 19, 1996

My last flight was Delta Flight 084/17 May B-767 ER Ship number N177DA JFK-MXP (Malpensa Milan, Italy) and Delta Flight 085/19 May MXP-JFK. The flight crew included Captain/First Officer Guy Gerard and Captain/First Officer John Grossweiler, Relief Pilot; they were two great guys who made my "Last Hurrah" a momentous occasion. It is a FAA requirement that every pilot has to be captain qualified to fly international flights over an eight-hour duration. The flight attendants consisted of eight under the leadership of Lio Baranta of Rome. They too "made my day." Also onboard was my second wife Hannah. My daughters had planned a reception for me upon my return to JFK; therefore, I requested the utilization of gate 14, which gave them a "bird's eye" view of the wet down. It is customary that two airport fire trucks provide an arch of water while the retiring pilot taxis the aircraft under the "Welcome Home Stream." The reception committee consisted of my two daughters, Linda Anne and her husband Jim and my youngest daughter, Leslie Anne, my Uncle Tom and Aunt Gloria and my first flight instructor with Northeast Airlines, Angus Perry and his wife Gen. Also present were my Aunt Gloria's twin sister Marie and her husband Angelo, who was like a brother to me since I was about ten years old. Some friends from New York and Florida rounded out the group of well wishers.

The flight across was a real great crossing and we arrived on time. The hotel accommodations were at the Jolly Touring Hotel, a few blocks from the La Scala Opera House. That night we dined at an Italian Trattoria named Mazuccelli, where the food and festivities were exceptional. The next morning we assembled at 09:30 for the trip to the airport. During the flight planning and briefing, I asked my two compatriots, who needed a landing and who wanted to fly home? This was my custom. They both refused to fly the trip back to the States. Normally, I would fly it over and one of them would fly it back. My guys stated that this was my day and that they were there to serve me. I had no choice except to fly home. Upon departure, the station personnel at Milan presented me with an Italian custard cake, which is my favorite. The standard procedure is to take off, fly over Lago Maggiore (Lake) and Lago Como and go into a holding pattern, since there was an altitude restriction of 24,000 feet or above to cross over the Alps of Switzerland and Milan is in close proximity to the Alps. We made two turns in the holding pattern and proceeded on course.

Our course took us abeam The Matterhorn, Geneva, Paris, London, Liverpool, Prestwick over Machrihanish and out over the Atlantic at N56.00.0 latitude and W010.00.0 longitude. We then proceeded to Goose Bay Labrador, then directly to Kennebunk, Maine directly to Providence, Rhode Island, direct to Calverton Long Island then radar vectors to overhead Roosevelt Field, overhead Garden City, Long Island landing to the southwest at JFK.

During the Calverton to Garden City portion, it got a little eerie for me. We were on radar vectors to the northwest at 5,000 feet and it took me directly overhead the cemetery where both my parents are buried in North Babylon on the south side of Sunrise Highway.

During the flight, my relief pilot, Captain/First Officer John Grossweiler composed a tribute to my ancestry, my multifaceted career and me. He read this to the passengers en route, which was quite moving and is included as follow:

The Public Address Announcement
for Retiring Captain Nicholas Gravino Jr.
By Captain/First Officer John Grossweiler

Delta Flight 85, Milan, Italy to New York John F. Kennedy International Airport, May 19, 1996.

"Today is a special day for us here at Delta Air Lines: Captain Nick Gravino, who is command of this flight, will be retiring from Delta when we return to JFK International Airport in New York. This is indeed most fitting; because he began his flying career in the New York City area.

His grandparents came to the United States through Ellis Island from Sicily, Italy almost 90 years ago. His family settled in the Borough of Queens, New York City where he was born and raised.

It was October 1965 when Captain Gravino began his flying career with Northeast Airlines, which became part of Delta Air Lines in 1972. During his more than 30 years of service, he has flown the DC3, the Fairchild FH227, the DC10, L1011, A310 and the Boeing 727, 757, 767. He is a genuine gentleman and spirited individual: It is indeed a pleasure to work for and with him: he will be surely missed at Delta.

We wish Captain Gravino and his lovely wife, who incidentally is accompanying him today, fair winds and following seas as they begin their retirement. They are both very active people whose next challenge will be to build their retirement home in Stuart, Florida.

On behalf of all our employees at Delta, best wishes to you."

Written by Captain/Relief Pilot, John Grossweiller
First Officer Guy Gerard.

Onboard were Mr. and Mrs. Glenn McDonald of Holtsville, NY who filmed the crossing and gifted me with a copy of the tape. Since then we have become real good friends. I appreciated his invaluable memento of my career and his contributions to formatting this book. We touched down at 14:52. Upon touchdown, I choked up as I came to the realization that everything that I had worked for over the last thirty-nine years had just come to an end.

Every air traffic control facility in the United States wished me well. Subsequent to clearing the runway 22L at JFK, we contacted ground control for taxi clearance to the Delta terminal, which was once the home of Pan American. We also contacted Delta ramp control for a gate assignment. The answer was gate 14, as planned. However, we were instructed to hold out of the entrance to the gate area, due to ramp congestion. I theorized that they had to set up the fire trucks; this was not the case.

It took about twenty-five minutes and we were finally cleared in to gate 14. Upon turning the corner to enter the gate area, we saw what the delay was, there was an electrical fine in the baggage claim area. There was Port Authority fire trucks, which are yellow. There were New York City fire trucks including hook and ladder trucks, which were red. There were Port Authority ambulances, New York City ambulances, Port Authority police cars and last but not least, New York City police cars. However, Tootey and Muldoon of Car 54 fame were not present. The area was covered with firemen with Scott Packs on their backs (Oxygen Breathing Apparatus). The Port Authority finally released one of the fire trucks so I only received one-half of a wet down. We pulled into gate 14 and I got quite nostalgic. I thanked my crew and all the passengers and shook their hands as they departed the aircraft for customs and immigration. My daughters and family had a greeting sign pasted to the glass enclosure at the entranceway to the jet way, which read, "CONGRATULATIONS ON YOUR RETIREMENT, CAPTAIN GRAVINO."

After clearing customs and immigration, I proceeded back to gate 14 and was greeted by my family and friends. I then had to turn in my flight manuals and in turn, I received many letters of congratulations from the CEO of Delta Airlines, Senior Vice President of Flight Operations, New York International Chief Pilot and a plaque for my thirty years of impeccable accident-free service.

We left the airport for a restaurant in Lynbrook NY where we wined, dined and proceeded to an evening of speech making and merriment. The next morning we departed for Palm Beach and a surprise party at my condo.

Thus ended my glorious thirty and one half year accident-free career that I miss dearly and will treasure every moment for the rest of my remaining days here on Earth, especially after writing my memoirs. The driving force through the years was as I stated previously " *the sorriest words of tongue and pen, are that it might have been.*" In my case, it was the greatest words I've ever learned. There were also quotes from a pilot's prayer entitled *"High Flight"* written by John Gillespie Magee, Jr. (included in the Exhibit section) and *"Oh I have slipped the surly bonds of Earth and danced the skies on laughter-silvered wings"* and to quote Mr. Francis Albert Sinatra, *"and did it my way."*

It has been an honor and a distinct pleasure that you have afforded me the opportunity to relive the initial portion of my life and to share it with you. To quote a dear friend of mine, Maxxi in Tumwater, WA *"thank you, thank you, thank you.."* There is more to come.

Chapter Sixteen:

Life Subsequent to Retirement
May 25, 1996 to the Present

I t took a while to get my finances in order. Organizing pension, trusts, health care benefits and pass privileges required an enormous amount of letter writing and income tax preparations.

I just received sad news that the Northeast chief pilot Paul Clancy who hired me was killed in an experimental aircraft shortly after take-off from Ft. Lauderdale Executive Airport. Paul was flying a 2/3 scale home built version of a WWII P51 known as a Stewart S51 built in Vero Beach, FL. I am quite familiar with this aircraft. I was very impressed with the rigid aluminum construction built to airline and military standards. I had spoken to the owner/designer and chief test pilot at the Stuart, FL air show. According to the newspapers, Paul's aircraft was equipped with a Chevy 454 cubic inch liquid cooled automobile engine that malfunctioned on take-off. Paul attempted to land on a parkway; he clipped two trees, the wings sheared off and the aircraft burst into flames. Upon further investigation, I discovered that the design called for the battery to be mounted between the wings dihedral and located underneath the pilot compartment. The definition of dihedral is the upward angle measured in degrees from horizontal in a fixed wing aircraft, measured in degrees from the wing root to the wing tip as viewed from the front of the aircraft. This is the lowest point of the wing section, so when the wings separated the fuel from the ruptured fuel cells flowed down the wing to the battery bus below the pilot causing the aircraft to burst into flames. This was a fatal design flaw, which eventually caused Stuart S51 to cease and desist. I am sure that Paul Clancy's estate prevailed in a lawsuit. My Mooney's battery was located well aft of the passenger compartment, eliminating that potential disastrous situation.

On various occasions during my aviation career when asked what I did for a living, I often replied that I was a heavy equipment operator giving the impression that I operated a diesel tractor or road grader, which I admit was kind of misleading. I enjoy my privacy and thus I would not be obligated to answer questions pertaining to the airline industry, which is normal for the average airline passenger. In September of 2000, while residing in Vero Beach, I decided to join the Vero Beach Italian-American Civic Association. This process required a sponsor. I chose a friend, Lieutenant Commander John Capra, who incidentally was the grandson of movie mogul/director Frank Capra of "It's a Great Life" and "Mr. Smith Goes to Washington." John received a Purple Heart while in Iraq during Desert Storm/Shield when his Jeep struck a land mine. In any event, the induction process consisted of an extensive background check, which lasted two months and required a unanimous approval at the induction meeting. There were a total of five of us inductees in attendance. We were advised to remain in an anteroom while the membership cast their yea or nay votes. The process took one hour. We were ushered into the grand hall whereby the president read a proclamation that we had been approved for membership. We took an oath and were sworn in. Upon completion of the ceremony we were each afforded the opportunity to say a few words about ourselves, i..e. where we were born and raised and what profession we chose as a career. The scenario went something like this: my name is Vinny Como si Chiama from Bensonhoist, Brooklyn. I was a bricklayer for thirty-five years before coming to Florida. This was the routine of my four companion inductees. I was last. I stated, "The name is Gravino and not Gravano, I came from New York City and I worked as a heavy equipment operator at Kennedy International Airport in Queens before coming to Florida.

To this day, they still don't know what I truly did for a living unless, of course, they read my book. So be it. Incidentally, Sammy (The Bull) Gravano was John Gotti's confidant who turned state's evidence against him.

Subsequent to retirement, I built two houses, one on a golf course and one on the Atlantic Ocean, which took a lot out of my marriage and me. Things were further complicated by two hurricanes, Frances and Jeanne in 2004 plus the loss of my sailboat named La Dona Sofisticata, which in Italian equates to "Sophisticated Lady."

Every year on St. Patty's Day (March 17th) Bill Donahue would have a ***"Fly-in"*** for all retired Delta/Northeast retired personnel at his airpark home at Ranch Colony Jupiter, FL. It is a great opportunity to get together with old friends and co-workers and reminisce times gone by.

In July of 2004, I was listening to some music at a local bar in Vero Beach, FL. There was a keyboard, bass and a drummer. During an intermission, the drummer approached me and said that he was taking instrument flight instruction at Paris Air in Vero Beach and had heard that I was a former airline pilot. We talked at length and I could sense that this young man had the *"**right stuff**"* to become a proficient instrument pilot. During the course of the next few weeks we became very friendly. He was quite interested in my lengthy career and enjoyed talking to me about some of my experiences, which I have been sharing with you, my readers, in this book. He was losing his self-confidence and I felt obligated to try to help him through these difficult times. I was there a number of times myself. I hadn't flown in eight years and had turned down invitations to accompany many other young aspiring pilots because the chemistry was not there. This was not the case with Dana Cyr from Swampscott, MA. Incidentally, Dana is one of the five top drummers in Florida and Massachusetts. I agreed that we would fly a simulated instrument flight from Vero Beach, FL to Daytona Beach, FL and return. I flew as his first officer and assisted him. We treated this flight as if it were a scheduled airline flight, utilizing all the standard airline procedures and call outs associated with the flight to the published altitude minimums for the approach into Daytona. The entire flight was textbook perfect and we flew back to Vero on the Atlantic Ocean and I took some pictures of my home on the Ocean. I would have enjoyed having someone like him flying for me with his enormous enthusiasm. It was a grand time had by all. Dana did a superb job and went on to get his instrument rating. Dana and I are still great friends, even though there is a thirty-six year difference in our ages. We have much in common.

On May 25, 2006, I turned seventy years old and joined the ranks of those seventy plus. As a loving gesture to my family, I decided to have a birthday party, given by me, the elder statesman, for my immediate family. I chose a restaurant on Long Island named Tellers situated in a former bank in Islip. In attendance were my two daughters, their mother Elaine, my two grandsons Michael James and Thomas Nicholas. There were also my sisters, Rose and Joanne and my niece, Denise and her two daughters, Julia and Sarah and her husband Jason. My nephews, Major Gary John and Andrew, my sister Joanne's sons, were also in attendance.

My nephew, Major Gary John, was the master of ceremonies and conducted the festivities. He presented me with two awesome gifts: a genuine US Air Force A2 flight jacket from my family, which was out of sight and a "cocked hat" American Flag with a proclamation (included in the Exhibit section of this book) stating that the American Flag was flown onboard his C130 for fifteen missions over Afghanistan in my honor. That presentation brought tears to my eyes and I will never forget the emotion it generated within my family. Gary John is quite special and so is his new wife, Erin. He resembles the son we lost at birth. In my eyes, it is a form of passing the Olympic Torch to a younger generation.

Chapter Seventeen:

A Captain's Guide to the New Hire Pilot

E tiquette and Protocol associated with an Aviation Career.

These are my views based upon my thirty-nine years associated with the pilot group. The new kids on the block will have a career of scrutiny from numerous groups and individuals, namely the FAA, the company, the traveling public, the news media, their families and their neighbors. My advice is to maintain a strict business relationship with all of the above and if you go by the book and buy my book, lol, you will never go wrong. During your first year, you are not under the protection of a pilot's union; therefore, I suggest you keep your eyes and ears open, maintain a high degree of professionalism and observe what is transpiring around you at all times. Become very analytical. I am not saying to not speak up when you see a problem. You will be flying with many types of personalities and people on different professional levels; therefore, diplomacy will come in handy, wherever possible.

There have been many improvements since I was a new kid on the block in 1965, thanks to CRM or as it is called, Cockpit Resource Management or Crew Resource Management. This deals with the polite way of conveying your observations to a superior without ruffling feathers too badly. Never discuss, in public, things associated with the airline or safety. You never know who is listening and who your passengers will be. My superiors were World War II types, or as I called them '*Supreme Allied Commanders*.' They consisted of either bomber or fighter pilots of an era gone by. It is said, RHIP or "*Rank has its Privileges*." Things are a lot more sophisticated today and the industry, as a whole, is much better educated.

As a captain, my philosophy, which I stated in a previous chapter, is that two or three heads are better than one. You might have seen something or experienced something that I have not. I believe in discussing the problem, time permitting and arriving at a solution, so that all parties concerned are in complete accord with the problem and remedy. However, the captain makes and is responsible for the final decision, especially if there is an inquisition subsequent to the incident. I would always prefer having someone testify for me rather than against me. I have learned that common sense must prevail. Here is a case in point. I have had situations wherein individuals got so wrapped up in the attempt to find and solve the cause of a problem, instead of the procedures to eliminate or reduce the effects of the problem, i.e., what caused the engine fire that they lost sight of the procedure utilized to put out the fire. This should be your main concern. You can't see the forest for the trees in a situation like that.

In this profession, one must be able to multi-task. The crew must have the ability to reduce or slow down the associated problems, so that they are handled expeditiously within the ability of the crewmembers involved. Be mindful of my favorite "situation awareness." You must not push the envelopes associated with aviation, such as, pilot capabilities, aircraft limitations and systems, crew resources and capabilities, ground support capabilities and equipment available. In a tense situation, use these to the max. Another bit of advice is *"don't mix business with pleasure."* Don't say anything that might get back to the wrong person… people talk. One thing that helped me during my career was to leave my career at the airport, not to bring it home into my personal and married life. Always keep on top of your finances and your future; wherever it may take you, be prepared.

You must develop a trust in the system. Having started working on the ground, I developed a wealth of knowledge into the inner workings of many of the departments that pilots are compelled to depend upon. I have flown with many people who seem to have personality changes as soon as they step foot on the airport property. They become very *"up tight."* One other thing... always have a " P*lan* B " and have an *"**Exit Strategy.**"* When in doubt, go around. I always looked out for my crew and my passengers. For this, I received many compliments throughout my career.

I hope this chapter helps you to put things into perspective and, possibly, helps in making your next thirty plus years with the airlines more enjoyable. May it also help you to redevelop the esteem that seems to have fallen by the wayside over the past few decades. Always remember *"pointy side forward and rubber side down" and "blue side up "* to *quote Captain George Chaudoin.*

HAPPY LANDINGS.

Postscript

Chapter Eighteen:
Required Reading

The Airline Passengers Bill of Rights

Airline passengers are entitled to *"Life, Liberty and the Pursuit of Happiness,"* or so they think while traveling… the not-so-friendly skies these days. However, this is not always the case. I will not belabor the issues, except to say, I suggest that you download an eighteen-page informative document prepared by the **United States of States of America, Department of Transportation, Aviation Consumer Protection Division.** This document provides the airline passenger with the tools necessary to combat any occurrence that may arise pertaining to his or her flight from point A to point B. There are fourteen items associated with airfares, reservations, baggage handling, delays and cancelled flights, contract terms, airline safety, just to name a few. This download also puts you in contact with the **Federal Aviation Agency** website and the **Transportation Security Agency** pertaining to the new and revised safety standards associated with carryon items. I highly recommend it; otherwise you will be at the mercy of the gods. The address is as follows:

Office of Aviation Enforcement and Proceedings
U.S. Department of Transportation
1200 New Jersey Ave, SE Washington, DC. 20590
http://airconsumer.ost.dot.gov

I have come across an incident, which I feel that every traveling passenger should consider prior to purchasing your next ticket on XYZ Airlines. During my career, it was customary for every airline to transfer the baggage of its passengers connecting with every other air carrier free of charge. Well friends, this isn't the way the cookie crumbles in today's world. This is one of those perks that have fallen through the cracks in today's **"Unfriendly Skies."** The rule is that the only way the airline with whom you book passage will transfer your baggage is if it participates in an **"Interline Agreement"** with the airline in which you are transferring prior to arriving at your final destination. If it does not, you will have to exit a secure area claim your luggage in the baggage claim area, have it transported to the receiving airline, re-enter security and start the whole check-in process all over again. By doing this, you will not make your close connection. According to the rules and regulations in existence since **Deregulation,** the airlines are not required to notify the unsuspecting passenger of the non-existent **"Interline Agreement."** Therefore, I strongly urge that every future passenger have this procedure tattooed to the top of the hand used for writing. This could really ruin your day and vacation. It is quite apparent that the airline industry has become a **"Mondo Cane"** (dog's world**).**

Many passengers and friends through the years have asked me, when is the best time to fly. My answer remains the same… early in the morning, basically the first flight of the day. This is because the aircraft overnights, the crew overnights and it gives the maintenance personnel an opportunity to do a thorough inspection. By scheduling early in the morning, you just about guarantee your flight will be departing on time. Of course, this is also dependant upon weather and ATC delays. This is a just a little food for thought to keep in mind when you plan your next trip.

Here are a few additions that will add a little humor into a very serious profession.

There have been numerous movies, such as *"**Boeing, Boeing**"* with Tony Curtis and Jerry Lewis, that poke fun at the relationships of flight personnel and the traveling public. There were also movies the likes of the original *"**Airport**"* starring Burt Lancaster, Jean Seberg, Dean Martin and George Kennedy as Joe Petrone. This was the first of a series of Airport and Airplane movies that were really not as realistic as the original. The aircraft decompression scene was, however, quite realistic.

There have also been a series of jokes that have evolved through the years and I have decided to add two, which are quite apropos and funny. The first applies to write-ups in the aircraft maintenance logbook, which is a legal document that records maintenance problems associated with that particular aircraft and flight. At times, there are quite a few humorous write-ups and replies and I have selected a few that just might tickle your funny bone.

After every flight, pilots fill out a form in the maintenance logbook called a "gripe sheet," which tells the mechanics about problems associated with the aircraft. The aircraft mechanics correct the problems, document their repairs on the form and sign off that the problem has been corrected; the next group of pilots review the gripe sheet prior their flight.

Never let it be said that ground crews lack a sense of humor. Here are some actual maintenance complaints submitted by pilots (marked with a "P") and the solutions recorded (marked with an "M") by the aviation mechanic:

P: Left inboard tire almost needs replacement.
M: Almost replaced left inboard main tire.
P: Test flight OK, except auto-land very rough
M: Auto-land not installed on this aircraft
P: Something loose in cockpit.
M: Something tightened in cockpit

P: Dead bugs on windshields.

M: Live bugs on back order

P: Autopilot in altitude-hold mode produces a 200 feet per minute descent.

M: Cannot reproduce problem on ground.

P: Evidence of leak on right main landing gear.

M: Evidence removed.

P: DME volume unbelievably loud.

M: DME volume set to a more believable level.

P: Friction locks cause throttle levers to stick.

M: That's what friction locks are for.

P: IFF inoperative in OFF mode.

M: IFF always inoperative in OFF mode.

P: Number three engine missing.

M: Engine found on right wing after brief search.

P: Aircraft handles funny. (I love this one!)

M: Aircraft warned to straighten up and fly right.

P: Target radar hums.

M: Reprogrammed target radar with lyrics.

P: Mouse in cockpit.

M: Cat installed

And now, I have saved the best for last.

P: Noise coming from under instrument panel. Sounds like a midget pounding with a hammer.

M: Took hammer away from midget.

Here is another one of those goodies:

A reporter for a local TV station requested that an aircraft be provided to take some live pictures of an out-of-control forest fire, for the five o'clock news.

The request was approved and the reporter used his cell phone to call the local airport to charter a flight. He was told that a twin-engine aircraft would be waiting for him at the airport. Arriving at the airfield, he spotted a plane warming up outside a hangar. He jumped in with his bag, slammed the door shut, and shouted, "let's go."

The pilot taxied out, swung the plane into the wind and took off. Once airborne, the reporter instructed the pilot, "Fly over the valley and make low passes so I can take some movies of the fires on the hillside." "Why?" Asked the pilot. "Because I'm a reporter with **THE TIMES** and I need to get some close-ups." The pilot was strangely silent for a moment. Finally he stammered, "So you are telling me…. You're Not My Flight Instructor? The moral of the story is, "Know who your Pilot is."

The War Against Terrorism:

Terrorism Strikes Fear into the
Hearts of the Bravest of Mortal Men

Terrorist attacks have been in existence since May of 1930, which was at the beginning of airline travel in the modern world. Here in America, this occurred on November 01, 1955 when a nut job put a bomb in his mother's suitcase and blew the airplane to smithereens to collect her insurance. The only thing that he collected was the executioner's lethal weapon.

After Fidel Castro came into power, the first American airliner was diverted to Cuba in 1961. In 1969, Arab terrorists hijacked a TWA jet bound for Israel and diverted it to Syria, which was the commencement of international terrorism of American Aircraft, as we know it today. This led to the development of the Sky-marshal program of the 1970s whereby armed Federal Marshals were transported on random flights. I will address only major terrorist events that have occurred. You may want to contact the US Department of State at www.state.gov/r/pa/pubs/fs/5902.htm, for a detailed description of terrorist activities throughout the years and throughout the World. The following events have had a severe impact on the peace-loving nations of the free world, especially here in good old U.S. of A.

Munich Olympic Massacre of September 1972

Entebbe Hostage Crisis of June 1976

The Iran Hostage Crisis of November 1979

Bombing of Marine Barracks, Beirut, Lebanon, October 1983

TWA Highjacking, Athens to Rome, June 1985

Pan American 103, December 1988

World Trade Center, New York, February 26, 1993

Federal Building, Oklahoma City, April 19, 1995

Khobar Towers Bombing, June 25, 1996

Empire State Building, New York, February 23, 1997

U.S. Embassy Bombing in East Africa, August 1998

Suicide Attack on the USS Cole, October 12, 2000

SEPTEMBER 11, 2001, Terrorist attack on the U.S. Homeland, WORLD TRADE CENTER, NEW YORK CITY DESTROYED and 3000 LIVES LOST. WE WILL NEVER FORGET.

The Bombing of the Pentagon and the airliner crash in a field in Southern Pennsylvania by Usama Bin Laden and crews

The killing of American Service Men and Women in Iraq, Afghanistan during The War on Terrorism, at the hands of Suicide Bombers.

These are only the tip of the iceberg. Use your imagination on the devastation caused by these faceless assassins.

Today, we and the other nations of the free world are faced with another enemy; the attempt by the Arab World to destroy our economy internally by increasing crude oil prices exponentially, due to our dependency on foreign oil. I estimate that by the summer of 2009 we will be paying $5.00 a gallon for gasoline. In the mean time... U.S. oil companies are on the bandwagon raking in enormous profits. It has destroyed the airline industry worldwide, the US economy, the housing market and the loss of American Military lives. I suggest we withdraw our troops from these countries and let them stand on their own two feet. The next American President must make this economic problem a major priority. Where is Michael Douglas, (who played President Andrew Shepherd in the movie "The American President") when we need him?

The Destruction of the World Trade Center, New York, September 11, 2001 and How It Could Have Been Averted.

O n September 11, 2001 at 09:30, I received word that two aircraft had penetrated the World Trade Center in New York City. Like the rest of the world, I was in a state of disbelief and did not comprehend immediately that it was an act of terrorism. I was fully aware of air traffic procedures associated with LaGuardia, Kennedy, Newark and New York Air Route Traffic Control Center. I was deeply concerned having worked for the Port of New York and New Jersey Authority, the FAA New York ARTC, and flown B767s domiciled at Logan International Airport in Boston and JFK in New York for Delta Airlines.

Many years earlier, while flying out of Boston, I came across a breach of security in the screening process, which pertained to the Kennebunkport home of President George Herbert Walker Bush. There was a regional air carrier that flew from Islip, Long Island to Boston and on to Portland, Maine that had violated the screening procedures at Boston's Logan Airport. I wrote a letter to the President pertaining to the problem and nothing was done to alleviate the problem.

The 9/11 terrorist plots were quite detailed and executed perfectly. They knew that the long haul flights out of Boston would entail B767 aircraft with a fuel load of at least six hours plus reserve. They were well aware of the idiosyncrasies of flying the B767 and the operation of its autopilot, which are on flight simulator programs and in published manuals, supplied by airlines of the Middle East countries, which probably trained the Al Qaeda Assassins. They could not activate their plans until the weather was VFR (Visual Flight Rules), which equates to CAVU, (Ceiling and Visibility Unlimited). They could not book their passage on those flights until they were certain that the weather was perfect, which would have been three days prior to 9/11. They were concerned not to leave a paper trail. Once they got airborne on the Boston departure, they had to gain control of the aircraft prior to reaching the Hudson River, which is the perfect route to New York City. Therefore, they had to strike just about the time the aircraft reached a cruising altitude of 35,000 feet, or about thirty minutes into the flight. The rest is history.

Airline pilot training procedures regarding this sort of behavior prior to 9/11 were very simplistic. They consisted of appeasing the high-jacker, who usually wanted to go to Cuba. Just don't make waves. There were no procedures in place to combat fanatical terrorists and the likes of Bin Laden or Mohammad Atta. The security of the cockpit door was non-existent. In fact, you could jimmy the door open with a credit card or kick it in with your foot. My friend Dana made a very valid point and I agree that security in today's world cannot be preserved, because of the fact that all flight crews have to leave the cockpit to tend to their personal needs, which includes a rest period on international flights. I very rarely travel these days, however, I ventured to Long Island, NY recently to partake in my grandson's sixth birthday. I had the opportunity to view first hand some of the new security systems onboard today's aircraft and have come to the conclusion that they are still inadequate. In my estimation, the cockpit area should be totally isolated from the cabin area. This should be accomplished by an airtight partition with a separate air-conditioning system, lavatory and galley with a door that can only be opened with the concurrence of both the flight attendants and the pilots. The pilots have a separate oxygen system, in case of a pressurization system malfunction. I noticed that adjacent to the cockpit door in the forward section there is always a lavatory; which means that, conceivably, the forward wall of the lavatory is not a secure wall and possibly could lead to a forced entrance to the inner sanctum of the cockpit. This just might be overly cautious; however, better safe than sorry and to err on the conservative side. There was no security camera system installed so that the flight crews could be alerted if there were serious problems in the cabin of the aircraft. I personally blame the FAA, the airlines and the pilots' unions for not taking an aggressive stance in the early 90s, such as Israel did against terrorists in the sixties and 70's. Weapons in the cockpit are a highly controversial subject. However, philosophies have changed, including my own. I would sacrifice my own life and those of a few passengers rather than my entire aircraft or the lives of all the unsuspecting individuals in those skyscrapers on the ground. They can say what they want; actions speak louder than words. I do not know what procedures are in place now as I have been retired for twelve years. Published Procedures in the Passenger Emergency Cards located on the pouch in the passenger seat in front of you must include combative measures, in the event of an attempted Terrorist confrontation. Had certain procedures been in place, 9/11 would never have occurred. My question to you is simple: " Why were *counter-terrorist procedures* not in place prior to 9/11?" Surely, there were more than ample signs and reasons to do so, i.e. The *World Trade Center Bombing* of 1993, plus the USS Cole. There are a series of switches and valves that control the pressurization on an aircraft. Had these switches been turned to the "off" position, the aircraft would have been depressurized in a matter of seconds. Everyone would have been confined to a seat, *Pull Down the Yellow Mask and Breathe Normally or Die.*

A radical procedure yes, but it could have saved thousands of lives. This would have rendered the terrorists inoperative, unless they secured a portable walk-around bottle from a crewmember. With all that confusion, they would have come unglued and human decency and **The American Way** might have prevailed. They as passengers would have been confined to a seat with a mask, or they would have died, lickity-split. It is pretty sad that these terrorists succeeded in overcoming the passengers and crews of the subject aircraft with box cutters, basically a razor blade with a handle. Envision this scenario: When terrorists with box cutters confronted the passengers, a male passenger could have reached into an overhead bin and brought down some carry-on baggage, briefcase, blanket or pillow as protection… the box cutters would have been rendered useless. And terrorist subdued by passengers. Why doesn't the TSA train able-bodied passengers, who are willing, in training these counter-terrorist tactics? Had instructions of this procedure been printed on the "Passenger Emergency Procedures" card, maybe the terrorists would have thought twice. Question, "Where is ICAO (International Civil Aviation Organization) or what has the United Nations done to help eradicate Terrorism?" Nada of course, this is all hindsight on my part. However, we have to get off our dead Asses and start using our heads because these terrorists are a lot more aggressive and apparently smarter than we are…especially than the congressional powers that be.

On August 16, 1999, I sold my beautiful home at Willoughby Golf Club in Stuart, FL and rented an apartment at the Fairways at Grand Harbor, Vero Beach, FL in preparation to building my castle on the ocean. The apartment complex was quite upscale with a pool, sauna, fitness center and the likes. The Fairways also became the residence of many flight students who attended the Flight Academies here at Vero. Incidentally, John Kennedy Jr. attended flight training here for his private license. One Sunday afternoon prior to 9/11, I was sitting at the pool and observed two young families, consisting of husbands, wives and six children. They were foreign and appeared to be Middle Eastern. The thing that was disconcerting is that I did not recognize the language. Subsequent to 9/11, I observed a photograph of this individual in the local newspaper and recognized the pool tile, as that of the pool in my apartment complex. There was also an abandoned auto in the parking lot with Flight Safety stickers on it. My inquisitive mind ran rampant and got the best of me. As a loyal American Citizen, I contacted the Miami office of the Federal Bureau of Investigation and furnished them with the information I had observed. Following 9/11 I did not see those families again. The FBI investigated my concerns and concluded that one the men was a Saudi Arabian flight engineer who was upgrading to pilot at Flight Safety and had no connection to the 9/11 massacres and that the car belonged to a Flight Safety student and was totally unrelated to 9/11. Better safe than sorry. FYI, any individual in any part of the world may purchase the flight simulator software, including the flight manual and the procedures on any aircraft, including the B767 and can become proficient to some degree on any particular aircraft. I have been able to practice landings and takeoffs of a F-18 Super Hornet on an aircraft carrier, which has been a dream of mine since my US Navy days, on my computer. As the saying goes, "Practice Makes Perfect."

The Death of Trans World Airlines

On July 17, 1996 at approximately sunset, Trans World Airlines 800, a Boeing 747-100 departed JFK for Paris De Gaulle Airport. The normal departure runway for jumbo jets is either runway 22R or runway 31L. In any event, the aircraft is vectored to the south until clear of the barrier island, which is commonly known as the Rockaways. Once off shore by some five miles, the aircraft is cleared directly to Nantucket VOR, (ACK), a radio navigational aid on Nantucket Island, and then directly to the vicinity of Gander, Newfoundland then an alphabetical track route consisting of latitude and longitude coordinates until approaching the shoreline of either Scotland or Ireland. The track from the south of JFK to ACK takes the aircraft about ten 10 miles off the southern Long Island coast. International waters commence at twelve miles off the coast. I have flown this route many times and since I was an air traffic controller at New York Air Route Traffic Control Center in the early to mid 60s and lived on the north shore of Long Island, I knew it would take me abeam my home in ten minutes at an altitude of 12,000 feet above sea level. This is consistent with the flight of the ill-fated TWA800, which attained an altitude of 13,800 feet.

I am completely knowledgeable of the disaster. I had spoken to TWA Captain Kevorkian's mother, Mrs. Flora Headley, who called NTSB's James Kallstrom a liar to his face and Captain Ray Lahr pertaining to his lawsuit against the National Transportation Safety Board et al. I thank him for his contributions to this section.

When I lived on Long Island a neighbor of mine was a Suffolk Policeman in the Fifth Precinct, which wound up responsible for the crash scene. My friend assisted in the recovery of the remains of the passengers, the wreckage, etc. Subsequent to the investigation and the findings, he advised me that there was an alleged cover-up on the part of the

NTSB. There was not just one hangar for storing evidence. In essence, there were two hangars, the Grumman Aircraft fabrication hangar and the paint hangar. The Grumman Aircraft fabrication hangar was for the parts and debris that the NTSB wanted the public to view. The paint hangar housed the debris, which included passenger seats that were impregnated with C4 Plastic Explosive material, etc. I contacted Captain Lahr to incorporate this evidence into his lawsuit against the federal government.

My theory pertaining to TWA800 is as follows. I believe a missile brought down TWA 800. It was either a terrorist missile fired from a ship in international waters, or a Navy missile accidentally fired from a warship operating in the Military Operating Area off Long Island. Terrorists had access to the hand held rocket propelled grenades used in the Iraq war, and the Navy or, possibly, a terrorist ship in International Waters had a variety of deck-mounted missiles. The Navy was conducting exercises and the warning areas were hot (in Operation).

It is common knowledge that the exodus to Europe commences at 17:30 daily from JFK and lasts for at least three hours, which would give terrorists a broad window of opportunity. This would last during daylight hours. In the late 1960s and early 1970s, while based out of Idlewild/JFK with Northeast Airlines, we would return about 23:30 from Florida. From Norfolk, VA to New York there was an endless row of lights from fishing fleets that were depleting our waters of precious fish and shellfish. A terrorist vessel could have easily blended in.

My facts pertaining to the NTSB's story of the exploding fuel tank is totally off the wall and if you believe it, I have a bridge to sell, and it is not that far from the disaster area. Based upon my training through the years, all aircraft fuel system designs and functions are basically the same except for some minor modifications. I will go through the similarities of the systems and then go into the B747 system. It will be up to you to judge for yourself and apply common sense to your conclusion versus the NTSB's version of what they want you to believe.

All aircraft fuel systems have circuit breakers that can protect and isolate the entire system. The circuit breakers are upstream of the switches that control the fuel pumps and the cross feed valves. Normally for an empty tank, these switches are off and there is no power to the pumps, switches and valves. Furthermore, the pumps and valves themselves are outside of the center fuel tank. Even the NTSB is not suggesting that the fuel pumps or fuel valves created a spark.

The only wiring within the center fuel tank is the wiring to the fuel gages. The fuel gages are normally left on throughout the flight. However, the fuel gages use a very low voltage and even if this wiring shorted to the frame, it wouldn't have produced an ignition spark. Furthermore, the fuel gages were operating normally, which indicates that their insulation was intact.

The NTSB really had to stretch to blame the spark on fuel gage wiring. The fuel gage wiring travels for a short distance in a wiring bundle where there are other wires carrying normal aircraft voltages. The NTSB is suggesting that there was a sudden interruption in the current of another wire in the same bundle, and that this induced a high voltage in the fuel gage wire, which breached the insulation and produced a spark hot enough to ignite the vapor in the tank. The analogy to this is the coil in an automobile that induces a voltage that produces the ignition spark in a spark plug.

Well, the coil in an automobile ignition system has a low number of turns in the primary coil and a high number of turns in the secondary coil. The ratio of the number of turns in each coil gives roughly the amplification of the voltage. Furthermore, the coil has an iron core that channels the magnetic lines of force through both coils. An automobile coil is an efficient transformer.

However, two insulated wires lying parallel to each other for a short distance are not an efficient transformer. It is highly doubtful that a change of current in an adjacent wire in the wire bundle could induce the necessary voltage and current in the fuel gage wiring. And, even if the voltage could be produced, there is no spark gap in the fuel gage circuit that is similar to the spark gap in a spark plug. It would take an enormous voltage and current to melt wires or breach the fuel gage insulation to produce a spark. This is where the circuit breaker comes in. If the circuit breaker is doing its job, any surge would pop the circuit breaker before any damage could be done. This is similar to what occurs in your home.

The NTSB has not produced any wiring from the wreckage showing incriminating evidence of burnt insulation or pits from sparking. Nor has the NTSB set up a bench test showing how such a spark could even have been produced. The fuel gage wiring spark is one more hypotheses plucked out of the blue with no substantiation.

The real clincher is that even if there was a spark in the center fuel tank, there wasn't a combustible vapor. Commander Donaldson referred to the fuel handbook and found that the temperature and pressure necessary for combustion just didn't exist. He performed a simple test with a pressure cooker to verify that the fuel handbook was correct. And, he sampled the fuel from the center fuel tank of a B747 that had been sitting on the ramp in conditions similar to TWA800. The fuel temperature was scarcely above the ambient temperature and far below the temperature necessary for combustion. Go to www.TWA800.com for a description of Commander Donaldson's work.

The NTSB sponsored a test trying to show that there was a combustible mixture in the center fuel tank. They had to add propane to their tank to get it to explode.

The center fuel tank of TWA800 did explode. However, it was ruptured and ignited by a missile.

I will now address the NTSB's theory of the aircraft's climb after the alleged center fuel tank exploded. Their theory based on the radar data and the flight data recorder was that, subsequent to the explosion, the aircraft climbed, which is nonsense. The nose section separated from the aircraft due to the explosion, which would cause the center of gravity of the aircraft to shift drastically aft, which in turn caused the aircraft to plummet to the Earth, tail first. Visualize that there are two people sitting on a balanced seesaw and one person gets off. What occurs? The seesaw becomes out of balance and, consequently, the individual remaining on the seesaw falls to the ground without gaining any altitude. The NTSB's theory is another example of the Government Administration's attempt to force-feed the American public into believing the *Impossible*.

In conclusion, had this been diagnosed as a possible terrorist attack coupled with the bombing of the World Trade Center on February 23, 1993 and other activities associated with Bin Laden, conceivably 9/11 just might have been averted. I blame it on the previous administration that suffered from *"cover-up-itis."* It was occupied with another crisis, namely, "Impeachment." I rest my case. If you would like to read some of the articles associated with this investigation of TWA800, I suggest www.whatreallyhappened.com/RANCHO/CRASH/TWA/twa.html or www.whatreallyhappened.com/RANCHO/CRASH/TWA/ 0_p.and www.press-nterprise.com/newsarchive/1998/07/17/9006548199.html. I would like to thank Captain Ray Lahr for his contribution to this section of my book.

It is about time we realize that the United States Government is in existence to persuade the American public to view facts as the government sees it and not to think for ourselves.

Deregulation:
The Rise and Fall of the Airline Empire, circa 1978

During the years prior to and subsequent to Charles Lindberg's trans Atlantic crossing, numerous aviation pioneers with visions of giant silver birds circling the globe were instrumental in forming the major airline system here in America in the 1930s and 40s. The likes of Howard Hughes, TWA, Juan Trippe, Pan American, C.R. Smith, American, Walter Varney, United Air Lines, C.E. Wollman, Delta, Paul Collins, George Gardner and Sam Soloman, Northeast Airlines, are just a few. These men and their co-workers formed an empire that lasted for half a century until smitten and toppled by The *Four Horsemen of the Apocalypse*, namely President Jimmy Carter, Civil Aeronautics Board Chairman Alfred Kahn, Senator Ted Kennedy and Senator Howard Cannon who succeeded in introducing the Airline Deregulation Act of 1978.

This act paved the way for upstart airlines like People's Express and New York Airways and Laker of England that would eventually cause Eastern, Trans World, and Pan American to cease and desist. Corporate raiders Karl Icahn, Frank Lorenzo and Freddy Laker were instrumental in the fall of an industry that I love dearly. *"The Donald"* emerged as CEO of the Trump Shuttle, which he purchased from the defunct Eastern Airlines and eventually sold to US Air. There were numerous CEOs with the quest for power and wealth, which would eventually, due to greed, bring these super carriers to the brink of disaster and beyond to Chapter Eleven and even Chapter Seven (total destruction of assets). The three major airlines that survived were American, United, and Delta.

I was a casualty of the Chapter Eleven filing of Delta Airlines. Delta Air Lines had great management under C.E. Wollman and Dave Garrett. Unfortunately, things went downhill, subsequent to their great leadership.

The retired Delta Air Lines Pilots' were the only Delta Air Line Employees that lost their pensions and their Healthcare and Prescription Plan.

Airline service has deteriorated drastically over the past three decades since deregulation as evidenced by the lack of comfort, amenities, food and beverage services with added surcharges. One other fallout from deregulation is the "spoke and hub" concept of air travel, requiring flights to airports not necessarily on a passenger's route of flight. This adds distance and time to a traveler's itinerary. For example, my sister was going to attend her son's wedding in Enid, OK and her final destination was Oklahoma City. She contacted Northwest Airlines who would fly her to Detroit from Hartford, CT and then on to Oklahoma City, which is quite far off the direct route as the crow flies. I eventually got her on Delta to Atlanta and on to Oklahoma City. She then rented a car for the trip to Enid. In my estimation, this concept adds unnecessary hours, mileage, fuel costs, and aircraft time to a person's air travels. This is counterproductive and costly.

Deregulation has been part and parcel to the demise of this giant industry, which I fear will never recover from this momentous set back.

I personally do not think, because of the ever-increasing cost of aviation fuel today, that mergers will solve the aviation industry's problems. It has to be solved from within, possibly using an alternative to today's jet fuel. Pulling our troops out of the Middle East and securing our borders just might cause OPEC nations to think twice before raising the price of crude oil. What say you?

Chapter Nineteen:

Topics of Public Interest: Areas of Great Concern

De-icing

I was often burdened with serious decisions regarding the safety of the passengers and of flight. While flying out of Boston and New York during the winter months, I was faced with the de-icing process pertaining to the aircraft. De-icing utilizes expensive equipment and a solution that has the consistency of a thick milkshake. The apparatus consists of a gigantic truck with an attached "cherry picker" to spray the horizontal surfaces of an aircraft with a heated solution of Monopropylene Glycol and hot water, a form of antifreeze, so that there is no accretion of snow or ice on the aircraft's surfaces during the take-off roll on the runway There are two philosophies and procedures in this area: the American philosophy vs. the European philosophy. The American philosophy/procedure is that the associated airline is responsible for the de-icing and it is done at the gate prior to taxiing out for takeoff. This can be very time consuming, costly and might require an aircraft to vacate its position in line for takeoff and return to the gate for a second application of de-icing solution. So it's not only time consuming but expensive, and includes the purchase of the associated equipment.

The European philosophy/procedure, however, is quite different and is as extremely practical and less expensive. It entails the following: the individual airport authority is responsible for de-icing all the aircraft at that particular airport. The flight is given a "slot time" for takeoff, as it is in the U.S. by ATC. Approximately forty-five minutes prior to the "slot time," the aircraft taxis to an area dedicated to de-icing. It is a specific bay, similar to a car wash, where the spent de-icing fluid is collected and recycled. Upon completion of the spray job the aircraft taxis out and takeoff with no delay. This procedure is especially economical, as the airline does not have to buy the expensive equipment, it is charged only for that de-icing and it does not have to be repeated.

I first encountered this procedure while flying B727 first officer for Northeast Airlines in and out of Montreal, Canada and it made a lot more sense than our procedure in the U.S.

The lack of this procedure was part and parcel to an Air Florida flight disaster on January 13, 1982, whereby, Air Florida 90 crashed on takeoff from Washington National Airport during a snowstorm. If you read the NTSB's accident report, you will discover that it was a multitude of sins responsible for the outcome, was attributed to *"Pilot Error." There was no excuse for not utilizing Engine Anti-Ice on takeoff.* The aircraft was on a taxiway for 49 minutes prior to take off, making it illegal for takeoff, due to the accumulation of snow on the aircraft and control surfaces. What were they thinking? No *Crew Resource Management.* Had this flight crew utilized European procedures, and the FAA approved *De-icing Procedures,* possibly and I say again, possibly, it just might have made it safely.

In 1985 I had a Salt Lake City overnight during the winter months. During those months, it is customary for the ski resorts in the immediate area including Park City, UT to pay to have the clouds seeded to produce snow. This was the case associated with my departure flight to Atlanta We arrived at the airport at 06:00, on his walk around, the flight engineer detected a light dusting of snow pellets on the horizontal surfaces of the aircraft and brought it to my attention. I went out to the jet-way and ran my finger across a cold section of a metal railing and noticed that it was quite moist, which signified to me that there was a good possibility it could freeze at any moment. I contacted the ground operations agent in charge and stated that I wanted the aircraft sprayed. The agent stated that they did not have any de-icing equipment available and that we would have to pay Western Airlines $600 to de-ice the aircraft. I stated, *"So be it."* Wake up America.

Prologue:
The Passing of Pat "Mother" Malone.

On August 12, 2008, I was sadly advised that at 05:01 that morning my dearest friend and mentor, Patricia "Mother" Malone made her *Final Approach and "Slipped the Surly Bonds here on Earth*," I muse she has traveled west... to God's Kingdom. Her new assignment may include instructing Heavenly Angels for the FAA (Future Angel Academy), developing operation specifications and flight time limitation for the Almighty's Aviation Cadets. She now answers to a *"Higher Authority."* Pat will be greatly missed by everyone who has had the pleasure of knowing this wonderful and loving, *Woman Amongst Women.* She is a legend in her own time and is irreplaceable. I am one of Pat's kids and I owe her a great deal. We love you and thank you Pat and will miss your *"Motherly Advise."*

Chapter Twenty

Exhibit Section

Introduction:

This is your Captain speaking.

The exhibit portion of this book is formulated so that you may accompany me on the chronological sojourn of my aviation career in the New York area and where ever else it took me. We have been cleared for take-off. Let us together "Slip the Surly Bonds of Earth."

HIGH FLIGHT
by John Gillespie Magee, Jr.

Oh, I have slipped the surly bonds of earth
and danced the skies on laughter-silvered
wings;

Sunward I've climbed, and joined the tumbling mirth
Of sun-split clouds--- and done a hundred things

You have not dreamed of--- wheeled and soared and swung
High in the sunlit silence. Hov'ring there,

I've chased the shouting wind along, and flung
My eager craft through footless halls of air.

Up, up the long, delirious, burning blue
I've topped the windswept heights with easy grace

Where never lark, or even eagle flew.
And, while with silent, lifting mind I've trod

The high untrespassed sanctity of space,
Put out my hand, and touched the face of God.

High Flight by John Gillespie MacGee, Jr.

High Flight

by John Gillespie Magee, Jr.

The following history of this Pilot's Prayer is from www.skygod.com.

During the dark days of the Battle of Britian, hundreds of Americans crossed the border into Canada to enlist with the Royal Canadian Air Force. Knowingly breaking the law, but with the tacit approval of the then still officially neurtal United States Government, they volunteered to fight Hitler's Germany.

John Gillespie Macgee, Jr., was one such American. Born in Shanghai, China in 1922, Macgee was 18 years old when he entered flight training. Within one year, he was sent to England and posted to the newly formed No. 412 Fighter Squadron, RCAF, which was activated at Digby, England. On 30 June 1941. He was qualified on and flew the Supermarine Spitfire. Flying fighter sweeps over France and air defence over England against the German Luftwaffe, he rose to the rank of Pilot Officer. At the time, German bombers were crossing the English Channel with great regularity to attack Britian's cities and factories. Although the dark days of the Battle of Britain were over, the Luftwaffe was still on the job of keeping up pressure on British industry and the country.

On September 3, 1941, Macgee flew a high altitude (33,000 feet) test flight in a newer model of the Spitfire V. As he orbited and climbed upward, he was struck with the inspiration of the poem- "To touch the face of God."

Once back on the ground, he wrote a letter to his parents. In it he commented, "I am enclosing a verse that I wrote the other day. It started at 30,000 feet, and was finished soon after I landed." On the back of the letter, he jotted down his poem, "High Flight."

Just three months later, on December 11, 1941 (and only three days after the US entered the war), Pilot Officer John Gillespie Macgee, Jr. was killed. The Spitfire V he was flying VZ-H collided with an Oxford Trainer from Crandwell Airfield while over Tangmere, England. The two planes were flying in the clouds and neither saw the other. He was just 19 years old.

"God bless these magnificent men and their flying machines."

History of High Flight by www.skygod.com

First Officer Nicholas Gravino Jr Northeast Airlines

Three Northeast Airlines DC-3 @ Montpelier, VT

Northeast Airlines B-727 295

Delta Air Lines B-767 ER taken by Alberto Riva

Sunrise over Normandy

Final Approach

My Last Flight Crew

19 May 1996

Dear Nick,

Today you turn over a page and start a new chapter in your
life. I just thought I'd contribute one of the pages for
you to turn over in your scrapbook.

I well remember the beginning. Here you were a low time
lightplane pilot embarking on a career with the airline. It
was that Douglas swept-winged racer, two engines and a tail
dragger at that. Those were the days when you couldn't
whistle and pee at the same time.

Your partner was a poor choice to be paired with you and you
were scared silly. Remember our Vic Tanney routines? Don
Bartlett didn't make it, as it should have been, but you
did. You were off and running.

Over the years I have kept tract of you and I well remember
the day in Port Jeff that I ran into you and spent a little
time clearing the air.

Nick, your friendship over the years has meant a lot to me
and I hope it continues as it has.

You will get used to retirement although it might pose a
little more trauma than you now expect.

Best of luck to you and yours in the days ahead.

Sincerely,

Eugene

Letter from Captain Perry

Mother Malone's Legacy

Angus and Me

Bon Voyage

Let it be known that this American Flag was flown aboard
an American C-130H aircraft providing combat support for
OPERATION ENDURING FREEDOM.
The 777 Expeditionary Airlift Squadron proudly flew this flag On
15 combat missions over the Country of Afghanistan
including the 11th of September 2003
for
Captain Nicholas Gravino
"Above all else, cherish that most solemn pride which must be yours to be
willing to lay so costly a sacrifice upon the alter of freedom."
— Abraham Lincoln, 1863

GARY J. PENNA JR., Capt, USAF
Aircraft Commander, C-130H 74-1674

CHRIS N. GARCIA, Capt,USAF
Copilot, C-130H 74-1674

MICHAEL R. MACALEESE, TSgt,USAF
Flight Engineer C-130H 74-1674

ROBIN D. MOREE, 1Lt , USAF
Navigator, C-130H 74-1674

CHRISTAN F. LEGUEN, AIC , USAF
Loadmaster, C-130H 74-1674

CORY M. EUBANKS, AIC, USAF
Loadmaster, C-130H 74-1674

A Captain's Proclamation

Printed in the United States
132314LV00003B/13/P